W9-CHX-071

Biznets

The "Webopoly"
Future of Business

Biznets: The "Webopoly" Future of Business
Copyright ©2006 by Frank Feather, Future-Trends.com, and Biznets

We acknowledge the financial support of the Government of Canada through the Book Publishing Industry Development Program for our publishing activities.

ISBN: 1-894622-61-8

Published by Warwick Publishing Inc.
161 Frederick Street, Suite 200
Toronto, Ontario M5A 4P3 Canada
www.warwickgp.com

Distributed in Canada by
Canadian Book Network
c/o Georgetown Terminal Warehouses
34 Armstrong Avenue
Georgetown, Ontario L7G 4R9
www.canadianbooknetwork.com

Distributed in the United States by
CDS
193 Edwards Drive
Jackson TN 38301
www.cdsbooks.com

Printed and bound in Canada

Biznets

The "Webopoly"
Future of Business

Winning Lessons and Strategies from
the "BIG 6" Online Stories
Amazon • eBay • Dell •
Quixtar • Sears • Tesco

by

Frank Feather

Best-selling author of
FUTURE CONSUMER.COM and FUTURE LIVING

Warwick Publishing

Contents

PREMISE
"Webopoly" Biznets 9
Web Lifestyles + Business "Webopolies" 10
Main Biznet Drivers 11
The "Zero-Infinity" Biznet Phenomenon 14
The "6 Ps" of Biznet Marketing Strategy 15
"Best of Breed" Biznet Webopoly Pioneers 17
The "Big 6" Online Biznet Exemplars 18
The Structure of This Book 19

BIZNET #1
Amazon: Biznet Pioneer 21
First-Mover Advantage 22
Obsessive Customer-Centric Focus 23
Personalized Brand 24
Leveraging Internet Technology 25
Automated Distribution Platform 26
World's Largest Product Selection: Way Beyond Books 28
Questionable Dot-Com Investments 29
A Web of Product Partners 29
Low-Price Value Proposition 31
Speedy Cash-Flow Generation 32
Conclusions and Outlook for Amazon 33
Strategy Lessons from Amazon about Biznets
and the "6 Ps" of Biznet Marketing 34

BIZNET #2
Ebay: Community Nexus 39
Virtual Corporation 40
First-Mover Advantage 40
Expanding Product Range 42
Category Management and Marketing 43
Obsessing about User Feedback 44
Web Lifestyle Community of Webpreneurs 45

Investment Mistakes and Strategic Partnerships 46
Leveraging Internet Technology 48
Auction Pricing and Fee Structure 49
Glocal (Global + Local) Multi-Channel Expansion 50
Conclusions and Outlook for eBay 51
Strategy Lessons from eBay about Biznets
    and the "6 Ps" of Biznet Marketing 52

BIZNET #3
Dell: Mass Customizer 57

First-Mover "Direct" Sales Advantage 58
Dell's "3D-Glocal" Biznet 59
Real-Time Manufacturing 60
Driving Down Costs 61
Cash-Flow Benefits 62
Product Range Expansion and Cross-Selling 63
Strategic Marketing and Customer Segmentation 64
Premium Attention to "Premier" Customers 65
One-to-One Customer-Focus 66
Strategic Customer Service Partnerships 67
Conclusions and Outlook for Dell 68
Strategy Lessons from Dell about Biznets and the "6 Ps" of Biznet Marketing . . 69

BIZNET #4
Quixtar: Webpreneur Franchise 73

Fast-Paced, Record-Breaking Start-Up 74
Highly Effective Web Site for Consumers and IBOs 75
"Ditto" Delivery to the Doorstep 76
Successful IBOs Earn a Large Business Income 77
Ideal e-Shopping Product Range 78
IBO Commission–Focused Value Pricing 79
High-Touch Mentorship + High-Tech Tools 81
One-to-One Community Relationships 81
Pre-Existing Biznet Infrastructure 82
Word-of-Mouth Franchising, Not Advertising 83
Undeveloped Marketing Potential 83
Emerging Hybrid Business Development Process 85
Conclusions and Outlook for Quixtar 87

Strategy Lessons from Quixtar about Biznets
and the "6 Ps" of Biznet Marketing. 87

BIZNET #5
Sears: Multi-Channel Hybrid 91
Sears.ca — First-Mover and Number 1 in Canada 92
Easy-to-Use Website 94
Catalog-Rich and Store-Wide Product Range. 94
Sears Canada Multi-Channel Infrastructure 95
Multi-Channel Shoppers Buy More. 96
Sears Roebuck and Sears.com 97
Lands' End Re-Energizes Sears. 97
"Virtual Model" and "Virtual Room". 99
Rapidly Expanding US Product Range. 99
Another Easy-to-Use Website. 100
Biznet Distribution System 101
Conclusions and Outlook for Sears 102
Strategy Lessons from Sears about Biznets
and the "6 Ps" of Biznet Marketing. 103

BIZNET #6
Tesco: "Glocal" Grocer 107
First Get It Right, Then Roll It Out Fast 108
Extensive Product Range. 110
Price Leadership: "Pile it High; Sell it Cheap" 111
Strategic Product Partnerships 112
One-to-One, High-Touch Market Segmentation 112
Supermarket TV 113
Profitable Home Delivery Process 115
Profitable within a Short Period. 116
State-of-the-Art Distribution Center 117
High-Touch Employee and Customer Service Focus. 118
Extremely Satisfied Customers. 119
Out-of-Touch Supermarkets 121
Safeway and Tesco in USA-Canada Online Partnership. 121
Conclusions and Outlook for Tesco 123
Strategy Lessons from Tesco about Biznets
and the "6 Ps" of Biznet Marketing. 124

Outcome: Biznet Strategies 129

Biznet Strategy Drives Corporate Strategy 130
Biznet Design and Operation 132
Winners Use the "6 Ps of Biznet Marketing. 133
Conclusion. 141

APPENDIX
Strategic E-Business Questions
to Brainstorm and Consider. 143

Index. 147

About the Author and Contact Information . . 152

PREMISE

"Webopoly" Biznets

Most North Americans will live a Web Lifestyle by 2007. And everything predicted about the Internet — even the most hyped thing — will happen. The winners will be the ones who develop a world-class digital nervous system.

—Bill Gates
Chairman, Microsoft

IF YOU SHOP ONLINE FOR BOOKS AT AMAZON, OR FOR PCS FROM Dell, you "get it." We are adopting the Web as naturally as a duckling takes to water, just like part of human nature waiting to happen — which it is. The Internet is us: we invented it, it is part of what it means to be human. It is our collective digital nervous system, and all of life and commerce are converging online.

Web Lifestyles + Business "Webopolies"

Today, more than a billion people worldwide use the Web, and half of them shop online. By 2007, 1.4 billion will be online and almost a billion will be e-shopping. In North America and other Web-advanced economies, the majority of people will be living the digital Web Lifestyle that Microsoft founder Bill Gates talks about and is described in my book *Future Living*: performing a great number of everyday activities via the Internet, from home or wherever they happen to be.

As media theorist Marshall McLuhan long ago taught, "The medium is the message." And the Internet is a global medium as central to people's lives as the telephone or television before it — and far more important and valuable. In the USA, it took thirty-five years for electricity to reach twenty-five percent of the population; TV took twenty-six years. It took PCs only sixteen years and the Web a mere seven years. Today in North America, seventy percent of households are online and they average more than two hours a day online during evening prime time. The TV era is ending and society is witness to the Internet Revolution, or "Webolution."

In parallel, this Webolution is creating a business upheaval where Web-based companies are growing to monopoly status. These "Webopolies" are leveraging the power of the Internet by creating real-time business networks (or "Biznets") that are transforming commerce in dramatic fashion.

As commerce and Web technology converge, companies are diverging between those that understand and exploit the Web and those that are either baffled by it or stubbornly ignore or dismiss it. Most companies still don't get it; many are being vanquished almost silently by stealthy groups of Biznet-savvy companies that align themselves with the same Webolutionary forces that are spurring consumers to flock online.

As a result, Biznets are grabbing market share, trouncing competitors, and deriving enviable profit margins. They are monopolizing Web commerce, which itself is gobbling up retail sales. For example, about 40 percent of computers and software are now sold online, as are about 20 percent of books. In many product categories, we are fast nearing a tipping point where the biggest online vendors will dominate their categories to become price and market leaders. In turn, their Webopoly power will drive non-Web competitors to the wall. Therefore it is mission-critical for every business to understand this new Biznet future.

Main Biznet Drivers

The Biznet future is driven by four main techno-economic megatrends. These trends are driving commerce towards "zero–infinity" Webopoly power, as follows:

1. Doubling every 18 months, at lower marginal cost

This is the business corollary of Moore's Law, which states that the number of transistors on a computer chip doubles every 18 months or less at the same price point or less. This law has held true ever since the chip was invented in 1971 and is considered by computer experts to be valid for at least the next decade — probably the next two or three decades, if not longer.

Indeed, Intel is intent on introducing a "multi-core" chip by 2008 that will be at least 10 times more powerful than the chips of 2004. These chips will perform an awesome 16 trillion operations a second, enough to stream vibrant multimedia content onto ever more advanced plasma screens. At the same time, each new generation of chips is less expensive than its predecessors. As well, the cost of broadband is dropping by 50 percent every 12 months, as is the cost of computer disk storage. All this technology is progressively more powerful yet cheaper and cheaper in cost.

The business parallel is that things that were technically impossible or prohibitively expensive become both possible and cheap. As a result, an optimally managed Web-based business or Biznet can double in size every 18 months and, while doing so, drive down its costs and thus boost its profit margins dramatically.

Simply put, only companies that totally digitize their operations will be digitally competitive in the new digital economy. The rest will shrivel and die against the blistering pace of digital Biznets.

2. Growing exponentially, with less investment capital

This is the business corollary of Metcalfe's Law, which states that the value of a network expands by the square of the size of the network. A network that is twice the size of another network is four times as valuable; one that is five times as big is twenty-five times as valuable. This occurs because the latest computer added to the Web is then "available," in a value-added sense, to all other computers already on the Web.

To further grasp this astonishing phenomenon, consider that there is a brand new PC switched on every second, around the clock. The billionth PC was shipped in early 2002. The next billion PCs will be delivered by mid-2007, each batch of them progressively more powerful than the previous batch. As well, there is a brand new cell phone activated every half-second, the newest of them almost as smart as PCs. Also, wireless chips are being embedded in everything from cars to fridges to heart defibrillators.

All of these devices are interconnecting in real time through the Internet and, as broadband spreads, are never switched off. People can transact and interact online at any time of day or night, wirelessly, no matter where they are: lying on a beach, sipping a latte coffee, strolling in the park, riding the subway, or flying at 35,000 feet.

The value of the Net thus grows as new people go online. And as it grows, its return on investment (ROI) grows exponentially because each additional networked PC yields more value than its proportional cost. Moreover, as noted, the cost of computing is constantly dropping, thus driving digital ROI even higher and generating abundant wealth for those who fully leverage the Net.

Economic wealth is created only from gains in productivity, and the Net is weaving a worldwide Web of wealth. It is an unprecedented global productivity machine that simply makes previous ways of life and commerce obsolete. Business has no option but to re-invent itself accordingly — and quickly — if it is to survive and prosper.

The network effect creates a growth momentum so overwhelming that, outside of a major management error, online success becomes an uncontrollable, runaway event. The exploding number of customers and the accompanying volume of sales reach a tipping point that flips the advantage almost irrevocably to the "first and fast" Biznet company in its sector. The economic value of the Biznet grows exponentially and the business becomes a magnet for still more customers.

3. Boosting value, by moving digital content faster and farther

This is the business corollary of McLuhan's Law, which states that electrified information reverses all previous processes and eliminates time and space.

In terms of reversal, online consumers clearly "call the shots" over producers. Consumers don't go to physical stores, the stores must virtually come to them. Products can't be pushed down people's throats; customers want to customize their own products over the Web. Products essentially become the content of the global Internet medium. Business thus must present its offerings to the consumer online, using the power of digital content.

The faster and farther you move digital content, the bigger and faster you build your Biznet and the more valuable it becomes. Hence, the best websites — that is, the most content-rich and user-friendly sites — attract ever more visitors. And those visitors tell other people about the site, and so its customer base grows exponentially.

As a result, when a Biznet company links together its partners, suppliers, and customers — in real time, anytime/anyplace — the economic value added for all participants is enhanced. Customers enjoy a comprehensive choice of high-quality, high-value, mass-customized products, delivered to the home. Thus satisfied, customers become repeat buyers who refer yet more customers, and Biznet sales and profits grow faster and fatter.

4. Extending reach, by being global + local + individual

With more than a billion people already online, the Net is a phenomenon of simultaneous globalization and individualization. It is a planetary platform, reachable by any company or individual anywhere.

Extending my own 1979 business tenet of "Thinking Globally, Acting Locally," the Internet allows any business, regardless of its size, to reach individual customers on a one-to-one basis worldwide.

Biznets are both "glocal" (global + local) and individually entrepreneurial. They localize their offerings and they tap into the natural desire of growing millions of Web Lifestyle individuals who want to do everything in their lives from home or wherever they are. This includes the desire not only to work at home but to own and operate a home-based e-commerce business. Millions of people already have become Internet entrepreneurs, or "Webpreneurs," and millions more naturally aspire to do likewise.

As a result of this megatrend, the world of commerce is diverging into two main sectors: a few glocal, mega-corporation, Webopoly Biznets, plus hundreds of millions of individual Webpreneurs — with little in between. In fact, some companies will achieve Biznet Webopoly status by building a worldwide franchise of home-based Webpreneurs.

The "Zero–Infinity" Biznet Phenomenon

Taken together, these socio-economic and technological megatrends imply that a successful Biznet can achieve what might be called an unassailable "zero–infinity" Webopoly position. To achieve this, they simultaneously drive down costs while rapidly growing the business, as follows:

Relentlessly drive down costs, lower and lower towards zero

A Biznet constantly lowers its customer-acquisition cost and can add customers to its database at virtually zero incremental costs. As well, its incremental inventory, transaction processing, and product fulfillment costs are lowered to a bare minimum. As an added plus, dominant branding is achieved without advertising, as Amazon and eBay have more than adequately demonstrated. Biznets also drive down product manufacturing and distribution costs through the extraordinary efficiency of digitized, real-time processes.

Exponentially expand market share, potentially towards infinity.

A Biznet's product range can constantly be broadened and the number of customers can potentially grow to everybody on the planet. Biznets are infinitely scalable; there are no physical limits to their reach and growth. Thus, for example, Amazon and eBay each already have almost 50 million repeat customers, and their respective customer bases and total sales are growing rapidly, as are their profits.

Such a zero–infinity Biznet, if it continues to effectively leverage every advantage of constantly developing Internet technology, can attract a consistent stream of new customers at minimal cost, maintain high profit margins, and achieve Webopoly market status.

The "6 Ps" of Biznet Marketing Strategy

Biznets are not just technology. They achieve exponential market growth by applying the "6 Ps" of digital marketing, which I will now briefly explain and summarize. In 1993, my book *The Future Consumer* predicted that the traditional "4 Ps" of the marketing mix would be transformed by the Internet into a "New 4 Ps" as follows:

1. Product becomes Mass-Customized Product

2. Place becomes Any Place + Any Time

3. Price becomes Dynamic Value Price

4. Promotion becomes Precise (1:1) Positioning

The initial years of the Webolution proved this "New 4 Ps" model valid. Then, in 2000 in *Future-Consumer.com*, I added two new "Ps" to the mix, making "6 Ps," for the following reasons.

On the Internet, high-touch customer service is increasingly paramount. "High-touch" personalized service is required to offset or counter-balance what otherwise might be a cold "high-tech" experience. This means we need a new "P" of "Personalized High-Touch Service." This concept thus closes the loop with customization. Indeed, to some degree, customization and personalization overlay all parts of the new marketing mix.

As well, website design and the entire online shopping experience is another critical element of brand interaction — one that in the Internet era is now much more important than traditional product packaging, product display, or advertising. Hence, we need to add a sixth "P" of "Profound Brand Experience."

The resultant "6 Ps" of Biznet marketing can be viewed in two inter-related systemic clusters — one focused on the product, the other on the customer — as follows:

Product "Value Web"

1. Mass-Customized Product

Built on-demand, in real time, to precise specifications — often by the customers themselves via a personalized website.

2. Any Place + Any Time

Ordered anywhere (locally or globally) at anytime ($24 \times 7 \times 365$); delivered to a PC or other digital device, or physically to a home, pick-up center, or store.

3. Dynamic Value Price

Dynamically priced, in discussion with the customer, often through an online bidding or auction process.

Customer "Experience"

4. Precise 1:1 Positioning

Real-time customer data collection and lifestyle profiling, to leverage lifetime value, via opt-in permission marketing.

5. Personalized High-Touch Service

A balanced high-tech/high-touch service that anticipates and enhances each customer's needs through personalized, customized solutions.

6. Profound Brand Experience

Brand interaction that optimizes buyer experience, ensuring a "bookmark" on the buyers' "Favorites" list.

The three product-related "Ps" are largely self-explanatory. As is shown by Dell or Amazon, these aspects of the Biznet marketing mix can be highly automated activities that the manufacturer and/or retailer is able to carry out routinely at low fixed and variable cost. The main point is to recognize that the linear supply chain is a defunct concept. Mass-customized products, e-channels, and dynamic pricing become interwoven into a "value web" that must function flawlessly and seamlessly in real time over a Biznet. It must be a truly friction-free network that the customer can take for granted as a reliable part of their shopping routine.

The three customer-related "Ps" require the most attention. The Web amplifies "word of mouth" through "word of modem." Hence, Biznet marketers must allocate more resources to building profound customer experiences. Much time and money must be invested in database marketing, customer relationship management, and website design — design that doesn't just create a website but builds a meaningful, distinctive, and compelling online brand presence.

"Best of Breed" Biznet Webopoly Pioneers

To demonstrate the above set of premises, this book examines six Biznet success stories.

Some so-called business web ("b-web") companies have been studied before. But most of them were companies that re-engineered and digitized their operations. They basically revamped their technology operations on an intranet to operate on a hub-and-spoke, web-like structure that, as our subject Biznets will show, is not sufficient. As well, most if not all of those b-webs were pure manufacturers with no real-time end-customer connections. Such b-webs are not comprehensive Biznets as defined here.

This book examines a core cross-sample of comprehensive Web-based businesses that are thriving globally in the rapidly growing online consumer marketplace. These six success stories are dominating their respective online shopping sectors. They constitute a new class of business model: "best of breed" Biznets that are pioneering the future of business.

These six examples automatically self-select themselves on the basis of the overwhelming consumer response they enjoy. After all, it is consumers, through repeat purchases, who reveal which company has the best business strategy. Online shoppers do so by popularizing one shopping website over another, thus quickly sorting e-business winners from losers.

Website success, of course, is not determined by consumer popularity alone; the website must be profitable or it will vanish. Given time though, popularity and profitability inevitably determine which sites come out on top. And it tends to be a winner-take-all market where the leading online company in a particular sector is far ahead of its main rivals.

But why do some websites win big, while others come in a distant second? What does it take to win online? What differentiates the winners from the also-rans? What lessons can other e-commerce aspirants learn from the winners? What can business in general learn from their success?

The Web has been around long enough for us to find answers to such questions. A few websites have clearly become much more popular than others. They must be doing something right. So which are they?

The "Big 6" Online Biznet Exemplars

The "Big 6" retail websites — all highly profitable — are, in alphabetical order, as follows:

Company	Product Category	Start-Up Market
Amazon	Books & Merchandise	USA
eBay	Auction & Merchandise	USA
Dell	Computers & Related	USA
Quixtar	General Merchandise	USA-Canada
Sears	General Merchandise	USA-Canada
Tesco	Groceries & Merchandise	UK

Other websites may dislodge some names from this list over time. For example, the world's number one retailer, Wal-Mart, was a bumbling and sputtering online starter but is finally showing some initial signs that it at least partially realizes there is a big difference between offline and online retailing. After all, any company doing one billion dollars a day in sales ought to be able to figure this thing out, and so cannot yet be dismissed.

As well, big shopping websites in countries with large, Internet-savvy populations — such as Rakuten in Japan, or Submarino in Brazil, or others emerging in China and India — inevitably will become huge on a global basis.

But today's Big 6 will be difficult to dislodge in their UK and North American home-base start-up markets. Moreover, these markets being where Internet retailing got started, they are a "first in class" sample of what online excellence is all about, how it might be improved upon, and what their Biznet models imply for business in general.

As we shall see, these big online winners ran fast and broadened their product offerings rapidly. All are volume leaders in their product sectors, and some are leaders globally and/or leaders across many product sectors in their national markets. As well, they all responded to online customer needs, which differ meaningfully from those of shoppers who actually go out to physical "brick-n-mortar" stores to make their purchases.

These early winners also consistently exploit everything the Web has to offer. They then build their business through word-of-modem recommendations among communities of consumers and by forming strong personalized relationships through customized offerings, exceptionally efficient product fulfillment, and customer-pleasing home delivery.

The online leadership position of these Biznets demonstrates key marks of excellence that account not only for their current success but for their survival of the dot-com shakeout of 2000–2001. Indeed, when everything seems to collapse like that, we need to examine what's left standing — and not only surviving but prospering.

In fact, the Big 6 Biznets emerged from the dot-com carnage unscathed, stronger and growing fast. This was not only because many of their rivals were weakened or vanquished but because these Biznets had a superior business model and excellent strategy execution. As a result, they are dominating their sectors.

The Structure of This Book

To show what marks Biznet success, the remainder of this book is divided into six core chapters — one for each of our Biznet exemplars — and a concluding section.

The six core chapters explore how each Biznet is, in its own way, re-inventing commerce. Then, for each Biznet, we'll develop conclusions and a bullet-point list of strategic implications or lessons that all businesses can learn from.

In the last part of the book, we'll draw out the common-thread strategies the six Biznets use to achieve Webopoly success. We will tabulate and compare how they developed, built, and now operate their Biznet, plus how they apply each of the "6 Ps" of Biznet marketing. Finally, we will list some questions for you to brainstorm as you consider which lessons and strategies you can apply to your own situation.

So let's begin with the Biznet pioneer, Amazon.

Amazon

biznet pioneer

Our business is not about selling
things. Our business is helping
customers make purchase decisions.
We establish relationships with them,
and help them sort through the
infinite shelf space of the Internet.

—Jeff Bezos
founder and Chairman, Amazon

AMAZON IS HISTORY'S FIRST DIGITAL GLOBAL RETAILING EMPIRE — the world's Biznet pioneer. The first to stake out prime e-commerce space in the Internet land rush, Amazon redefined how people consume products and services. The Web's largest retailer, it is rewriting the rules of retailing. And perhaps more than any other online company, it is defining what e-business is all about, and what it takes to be successful in the new Web-based business world. Any business — large or small, online or offline — can learn from Amazon's trailblazing path to success.

First-Mover Advantage

The future belongs to those who get there first. And one of the keys to digital business success is the "first-mover advantage," where one company gets a jump-start on any potential competitors and tries to "get big fast."

Amazon embodies this concept. It opened a very simple website in 1995, very quickly became an e-commerce legend, and today it offers "Earth's Biggest Selection" of products. From the start, the company has been number one in online brand recognition.

Jeff Bezos pioneered online shopping in the same way that Sam Walton pioneered big-box retailing with Wal-Mart. The impact was so dramatic that, at the height of the initial dot-com surge, *Time* magazine named Bezos "Man of the Year" for 1999.

Some have said that Amazon is the Wal-Mart of the Web; that it is "Wal-Marting" the Web. This is a wrong analogy. For its part, Wal-Mart so far is doing very poorly on the Web because, as noted earlier, it clearly does not yet grasp how the Web changes retailing. Indeed, Bezos does not see Wal-Mart as competition, telling *Business Week* in 2002 that "the set of skills and competencies to be a superb physical world retailer are completely different from those you need to be a superb online retailer."

But Amazon could be seen as the number one department-store anchor tenant in Earth's biggest shopping mall, the Web. Amazon is, after all, the very first place where almost every online shopper goes to make a digital purchase. And then they keep on coming back.

Unlike Wal-Mart, which made a profit in its first year of brick-n-mortar retailing, Amazon started out losing money. But Walton was able to develop his chain of stores quietly, starting in the out-of-the-way state of Arkansas. Bezos' original but oft-maligned vision was that the Internet offered such a revolutionary new business platform, only companies that became big fast, while ignoring short-term profitability, would survive and prosper. In his first "Letter to Shareholders" in Amazon's 1997 annual report, Bezos explained his fast-growth strategy as follows: "We will continue to invest aggressively to expand and leverage our customer base, brand, and infrastructure to establish an enduring franchise." Profitability was not a key metric.

He kept his focus and turned out to be right. By 2002, Amazon buried any doubts about the company's viability and has since grown in profitability every quarter. That year Bezos said, "We're still at the very beginning; there's much more to come." And he's been right about that too. The main reason is, as the digital pioneer, Amazon is destroying the traditional retailing value chain. Its Biznet infostructure is a huge economic growth engine that transforms unique customer service capabilities into shareholder value.

Obsessive Customer-Centric Focus

One of Amazon's biggest advantages today is that it knows more about online shoppers, simply because it has been serving them longer and better than anyone else. Amazon is number one in online customer service rankings, according to the University of Michigan's American Customer Satisfaction Index, enjoying the highest-ever ratings of any company, regardless of industry. In 2004, Amazon ranked number one overall in another survey of "customer respect." And the gap between Amazon and its competitors is likely to continue to widen as it executes superbly and continues to add to its huge base of extremely satisfied customers.

Amazon also understands how the Internet changes the shopping process. Media guru Marshall McLuhan long ago foretold that the speed-up of electrified information would "reverse all processes." In the case of modern-day shopping, you don't go out to a public store; it comes to you — online — and becomes your private shop. In 1998, Bezos astutely told *Business Week* magazine, "We want Amazon to be the right store for you as an individual. If we have 4.5 million customers, we should have 4.5 million stores." Bezos saw the reversal: that the Web shifts power from producers to consumers. Product distribution shifts from "push" to "pull"; the customer decides. Retailing shifts from being a supplier-driven product business to a buyer-driven service business.

Bezos also said, "You take customers and put them at the center of their own shopping universe." In turn, Amazon's vision is "to be the world's most customer-centric company; a place where customers can find and discover anything they might want to buy online." For example, the website's Friends & Favorites area lets customers help each other find products. Features such as the "About You" pages, discussion boards, purchase circles, and refer-a-friend, transform customers into their own website content, and thus enrich their shopping experience. Amazon depends on positive customer experiences for much of its growth because it does not advertise but rather depends on word-of-modem publicity.

Today, Amazon has 44 million-plus repeat customers — that is, 44 million-plus virtual retail outlets. It places millions of available products into those virtual stores, which are conveniently located on each of its 44 million-plus customers' home computers; Amazon brings the products to them. Customers do not need to go anywhere to shop; they "pull" up the products they want onto their PC screens, thanks to Amazon's personalization feature, which provides one-to-one, customized storefronts to suit the precise tastes of every customer.

Personalized Brand

Personalization reinforces Amazon's brand and implies that the brand means different things to different people. For example, the link to Amazon's website on my Favorites list is in fact a link to *my* Amazon. As a 1999 article in *Brandweek* observed, when shoppers customize their own interface, they "set the brand's parameters and agenda." And when that brand experience exceeds their expectations, consumers eagerly will use it again and will recommend the brand to others. Amazon thus created a meta-brand or what some leading-edge advertising people now call a "love mark." People love Amazon.

Contrast this with the impersonal nature of mass merchandising. Even the most cavernous big-box store has limited shelf space, for which manufacturers clamor. And both manufacturer and retailer are under pressure to sell what they have in inventory. But the Web has infinite shelf space, and digitized production and distribution means that items can be mass-customized very quickly, thus reducing the need for inventory. Amazon leverages the Internet's exponential economies of scale, where customers have better information and can comparison-shop quickly and easily. Amazon also is a place where customer reviews and customer-to-customer product endorsements accelerate and proliferate via e-mail and instant messenger services.

Amazon capitalized on these and other features of the Internet to create the first truly Internet brand and then extend it across global markets and multiple product categories. It offers personalized shopping with a global reach that no competitor can match. Now almost a monopolistic, perpetual-profitmaking Biznet, the barriers of entry into its retail space are formidable. In fact, Bezos envisions multiple, always-on computers in every home that will drive Amazon's business growth to infinity.

Leveraging Internet Technology

The Internet allows Amazon essentially to be an information-based business or a content supplier. It brokers information about products to potential buyers and info-manages its Biznet (manages its business through the power of instantly available, real-time information) to serve customers. It does not so much sell books and other products as provide customized information *about* books and other products. Its product search feature takes customers to products with exacting precision and speed. Then the product is enhanced with information such as technical details, product reviews, and (in the case of books) even excerpts that can be read or searched for content.

Ordering takes place via a secure "1-Click" shopping cart that remembers all the customer's details (name, address, credit card numbers), ready for the next time they use their account. This information base enables Amazon to suggest other products (that is, attempt to cross-sell them), based on previous purchase choices, the next time the customer visits the site. Indeed, customers can tell Amazon which kinds of products most interest them and can develop "wish lists" of gift items they would like to receive.

This is all achieved through a technique called "collaborative filtering" that analyzes data generated by each customer's product searches, purchases, and suggestions. Searches and purchases implicitly infer a person's product tastes; actual orders confirm those tastes.

Upon ordering, customers receive an instantaneous e-mail confirming the order. Shoppers also are able to track or change their order at any time by simply logging back into their account. Every transaction is 100 percent satisfaction guaranteed: Amazon customers pay nothing if unauthorized charges are ever made to their credit cards. It doesn't happen.

This exemplifies Amazon's extraordinary level of customer service and support. The site offers comprehensive help files and a menu of dedicated e-mail addresses to handle customer feedback and queries, each of which again receive prompt responses and solutions. Customers also can review products, submit suggestions, and point out any errors in product listing information.

Amazon continually introduces new features — such as the "1-Click" checkout, personalized recommendations, the "Search Inside the Book" option, its own A9.com search engine, or wireless shopping via handheld devices — all designed to build customer relationships and drive a one-to-one customer experience.

Amazon's Biznet platform thus exploits Internet capabilities and related software to the hilt. Like almost everything else about Amazon, the easy-to-use functionality, features, and responsiveness of the website are second to none. In fact, as discussed later, Amazon's platform is so good that other companies are now partnering with Amazon to have their products distributed through it.

Automated Distribution Platform

Amazon also leverages the Internet to offer extraordinary product fulfillment. Bezos started the company out of his garage in Seattle, wrapping orders himself and driving them to the post office in his car. That personal touch continues to drive customer satisfaction, even though Amazon's technology platform and product distribution system has grown to an enormous size.

To physically deliver the product, Amazon built the Internet's first warehouse distribution network specifically designed to send out merchandise on an item-by-item and customer-by-customer basis. (Quixtar Corporation, discussed later in the book, was fortunate in being able to use a similar distribution system already established by a sister company.) As customers order an item from Amazon — any and all of which are both non-perishable and easily conveyable — conveyor belts automatically slide items into a customer-dedicated cubby in the distribution center.

From there, items are gathered up and packaged for shipment. Amazon thus can ship single items, from a selection of tens of millions, to any individual among its tens of millions of customers. It is a perfect example of one-to-one, mass-customized marketing and distribution which only a Biznet allows.

During the 2004 year-end shopping rush, for example, Amazon set a single-day global sales record for itself of 2.8 million units shipped, or 32 items per second. Visitor traffic peaked at 700,000 users during one 60-minute period. During the entire 2004 US Thanksgiving–Christmas sales period, for example, Amazon sold an average of one watch every minute, demonstrating how well a Biznet can sell single products to single users.

From books to electronics to watches, Amazon's distribution system is so scalable it can potentially handle about 10 times as much volume as now. It can keep minimal quantities in inventory and yet make products available to an entire continent, restocking as quickly as customers order. And, unlike brick-n-mortar retailers who must invest in new stores to build revenues, Amazon can boost sales by simply tweaking its software to broaden its product offerings and customer service.

The capital-intensive real estate model of brick-n-mortar retailing cannot even come close to such economic leverage. Even worse, a brick-n-mortar retailer may fail to integrate its offline and online operations. For example, Barnes & Noble set up its online operation as a separate entity. Neither the offline nor the online operation could capitalize on the synergies that would flow from an integrated "click-and-mortar" Biznet hybrid.

World's Largest Product Selection: Way Beyond Books

At first, Bezos wanted Amazon to become "Earth's Biggest Bookstore." But he always envisioned the site as much more than that. After opening its virtual doors with 1.1 million book titles (10 times that of the largest bookstores), Amazon leveraged that edge and its ever-growing customer base into other retail product categories ideal for online merchandising.

In this way, Amazon extended its brand name across the retail spectrum to become a place to shop online for almost anything. This not only locked out other book sellers, it raised huge barriers to entry for other product retailers who wanted to open up an online channel. Amazon geared up fast to offer an ever-increasing selection of products that were easy to find.

Amazon thus quickly moved into other easy-to-buy-online items like music and videos. Such was its power that it became the number one music retailer within three months and the dominant video retailer within one month of offering the products. Then it added a slew of electronic products, such as cameras, computers, software, TVs, and CD players. By then, book title offerings had grown to 4.7 million.

Other product selections were added at a fast and furious pace and Amazon today sells everything from apparel and appliances to sporting goods and toys. In fact, during the 2004 year-end shopping spree, consumer electronics surpassed books as Amazon's largest sales category. The book business also posted record sales, but Amazon's electronics sales show that it can diversify beyond books and videos, even though that combined "media" category still represents about 70 percent of Amazon's total annual sales.

The expansion of electronics sales was achieved through lower prices and also from deeper digital product content, including thousands of product manuals that can be freely downloaded from the site. A related innovation, started in 2004, is to show short (five- to ten-minute) online movies, with links to products just seen. Clicking the names of actors and directors takes you to their "boutiques" to buy other videos, or apparel, furnishings, cosmetics, electronics, and jewelry used in the movies.

Amazon thus has built a massive online shopping mall that differs greatly from most other big online sites. For example, Yahoo and AOL are huge portals that mostly send visitors to the websites of online retailers in exchange for commissions. These are not Amazon-like shopping sites: they don't offer one-stop shopping and they don't have a dedicated base of loyal customers who get personalized and customized online service. As a result, online shoppers are shifting from portals to one-click Biznets like Amazon.

Questionable Dot-Com Investments

I am not saying that Amazon hasn't made its fair share of mistakes. In a fast-track rush to broaden its product range, it went on a buying spree in the dot-com frenzy to acquire large chunks of upstarts such as Pets.com, Gear.com, HomeGrocer.com, and Drugstore.com.

Basically, all of these were bad investments. For many such dot-coms, it was just too early. Some of the models didn't work, or they could not scale up fast enough. They will eventually come back as second-phase Internet opportunities, but not until later this decade.

Also, in an ill-fated attempt to compete with eBay in the auction and private entrepreneur segment, Amazon invested in LiveBid.com and launched its zShops virtual mall in 2000 where any seller could set up an electronic storefront at Amazon.com. While there are now almost one million zShops at Amazon, eBay had a giant first-mover advantage in this space and Amazon could never seriously compete with it.

A Web of Product Partners

To its credit, instead of these somewhat misplaced efforts, Amazon turned its energies to building an adjunct network (an extended Biznet) of brand-name partner stores.

Amazon has become a Biznet technology service provider. Through a new subsidiary called Amazon Services, it leverages its superior Biznet platform and exceptional customer service reputation by, in effect, leasing out its Biznet to other product retailers.

In 2000, for example, Amazon formed a 10-year partnership with ToysRUs to present a co-branded offering where the two companies leverage their respective areas of expertise. ToysRUs manages toy procurement, inventory, and merchandising, while Amazon manages the front-end online store, product fulfillment, and customer service, with Amazon basically earning a commission on all the volume it handles. In entering this arrangement, ToysRUs effectively admitted its own online failure, showing how difficult it is for brick-n-mortar retailers to make the transition to the online channel.

A year later, Amazon won an even more symbolic victory when Borders Books, the second-largest brick-n-mortar book retailer, closed its online channel (after a three-year struggle) to partner with Amazon instead. Borders.com was re-launched as a co-branded website powered by Amazon's Biznet platform. Amazon shares the revenue, and customers can either have the books shipped or arrange to pick them up at a Borders or a Waldenbooks store (Walden is owned by Borders).

Other brand-name companies outsource their Web operations to Amazon, and also sell their products at Amazon as well as on their own websites, under a variety of similar arrangements. They include Target, Gap, Foot Locker, Office Depot, Nordstrom, Circuit City, Sony, Virgin Entertainment, Eddy Bauer, Bombay, ELuxury (a division of MH Louis Vuitton), and Lands' End (now a division of Sears, discussed in a later chapter).

Amazon even provides links to websites of other companies' products. For example, a customer searching on Amazon for computers might be shown a link to Circuit City's shopping site. If the customer subsequently buys there, then Amazon receives a commission for the referral. Similarly, a query for a bread maker might take the shopper to the Williams-Sonoma site. In short, if Amazon can't supply the product, it's just as happy so long as one of its partners can.

These companies partner with Amazon for a fee estimated to be about 10 percent or more of retail product value. By 2002, it was estimated that about 25 percent of Amazon's total sales came from these third-party sellers, a figure that by 2004 was about 30 percent and growing. The bulk of these revenues are mostly clear profit in that the costs of Amazon's fulfillment and customer service systems are already absorbed by Amazon's overall operation. Many analysts forecast that such revenue could account for 50 percent of Amazon's total revenue by 2008.

Such arrangements speak volumes about the excellence of Amazon's Biznet (many of these partners switched to Amazon from some of the major online portals) and the inability of otherwise successful retailers to enter the digital domain.

Through such synergistic arrangements, Amazon is able to expand into different product categories without making an investment in inventory. Nor does it have to forecast fluctuating product demand in unfamiliar and trendy product categories, nor handle pesky product returns. All of this is handled by the partner stores. In return, the partners gain access to Amazon's most valuable assets: its Internet know-how, its billion-dollar Biznet, and its 44 million-plus active shoppers.

Low-Price Value Proposition

Ease of product selection and competitive pricing are the two prime motivators of online shoppers worldwide. Indeed, the Internet allows online shoppers to easily and quickly make price comparisons between products. Success goes to those companies that build efficiencies of scale to keep costs low so they can offer deeper discount prices than competitors.

Jeff Bezos has repeatedly said, "There are two kinds of retailers: those that work to raise prices; and those that work relentlessly to lower them. We are firmly committed to lower prices. It's all about selection, convenience, and lower prices."

The cost of shipping also is a big concern for online shoppers and is the main reason why they abandon their shopping carts without completing their order. To encourage larger customer orders, Amazon has constantly reduced its shipping charges and now offers free shipping on orders above a minimal value.

The incremental cost of shipping one more item on an order is far less than the cost of fixed investments in warehouses, technology, and in-store shelf space by competitors. Free shipping amounts to a mere two percent of Amazon's total sales revenues, significantly less than retailers might spend, for example, on advertising. As the biggest e-commerce brand, Amazon has little need to advertise. In fact, it says it gets a better return by investing in lower prices than it does by advertising.

Only one or possibly two companies can effectively be an industry's low-price leader. Others wishing to compete in their market must bring a unique value offering. Amazon has thus created a huge barrier to entry with its low-price and free-shipping strategy. It believes that saving the customer money will improve the customer experience and boost sales.

That strategy seems to be effective. Even though Amazon's customers are some of the more upscale on the Web, with a median household income of $77,000 (as of 2002), they tend to be active online shoppers who are attracted to Amazon's value proposition. They return there again and again, spend at least 10 percent more online than the average e-shopper, and their average order size is constantly increasing.

But is low-price leadership and free shipping a sustainable strategy? According to Bezos, "The answer is pretty clear: It is one of the best ways to create a sustainable strategy. There's a productivity increase as you get more scale. You can lower prices and also get more fixed-cost leverage. It is a sustainable strategy, as great companies like Wal-Mart demonstrate."

Speedy Cash-Flow Generation

However, big-box retailers such as Wal-Mart need to carry 160 days' worth of inventory and must pay suppliers within 45 to 90 days. They thus carry inventory for up to four months. Amazon dramatically reverses that typical business cash-flow conversion model. It charges the customer's credit card as the order is shipped, thus collecting sales revenues before it has to pay product distributors (such as book publishers and electronics manufacturers) as much as 60 days later. Amazon's inventory turns over in less than 20 days, thus giving it 40 days' free use of the cash, which runs at about a million dollars a day.

Amazon is a huge cash-flow generator. In 1995, its first year, Amazon sold just $511,000 worth of merchandise. In 2000, it sold $2.8 billion worth of goods, but reported a net loss of $1.4 billion. By 2002, however, Amazon became profitable and is now growing its bottom line quickly. Sales in 2004 approached seven billion dollars and the company projects around eight billion dollars for 2005 —

half of it from outside North America. Net profit is running at more than $350 million a year and growing rapidly as the worldwide customer base expands and as those customers buy more items.

Conclusions and Outlook for Amazon

Amazon has proven that if you can build a big enough online-customer base and serve it with excellence by exploiting the Web's technology, all while managing infrastructure and marketing costs against revenue growth, then profitability is sure to follow.

The first-ever online book sale occurred soon after Amazon launched in July 1995. By 2000, online book sales captured six percent of the entire market. In 2004, nineteen percent of books were sold online, and the percentage continues to grow. Ten years on, it is hard to imagine that Amazon started out as a tiny online "order taker" for books, shipping them out of a family garage in Seattle. It has established its place as the world's pre-eminent Internet retailer with growing markets across all continents.

How did Amazon achieve this remarkable success?

Amazon was founded by a visionary leader who was prepared to navigate virgin retail territory. It enjoyed first-mover advantage in a brand new retailing channel. It saw a large and rapidly growing market opportunity. It rapidly created a great brand name by being the "poster child" for e-commerce. It reinforced that brand by investing heavily and generating enough cash flow and market growth to stay ahead of its debt load.

It quickly became the hands-down market leader in Web technology and online marketing, with the best personalization of the online shopping experience of any retailer. To add to its own product offerings, it built a network of partnership sellers of established brand-name merchandise. Its website attracted happy customers who told their friends about a fantastic online shopping experience.

Online shoppers place Amazon atop their website Favorites list and return there routinely. In fact, Amazon is the Internet's most-visited shopping site, attracting a monthly audience of 29.8 million visitors globally. This number increases daily as more people go online for the first time. It increases further, as do sales, once those users get broadband Web access.

The mind boggles at what will happen to Amazon's sales once most of the world's consumers are online (it's already 70 percent in North America), all with broadband access to make shopping easier (already 50 percent of North American Web users have broadband), and are frequent online shoppers (already 70 percent of North American Web users).

Moreover, by then, it is inevitable that Amazon will have improved its website even more, and will have many of the world's best brands as partners sharing its Biznet platform, thus broadening the product offering to hundreds of categories.

By 2010, Amazon could have a billion active customers, each buying an average of at least $1,000 of product a year — you do the math! This truly is the 21st-century "Amazonian giant" of online retailing.

Strategy Lessons from Amazon about Biznets and the "6 Ps" of Biznet Marketing

Biznet

- Set a visionary and audacious goal, and never lose sight of your purpose.

- Be a "first-mover" and scale up fast to raise huge barriers to entry.

- Quickly build a critical mass of loyal customers; cultivate long-term relationships.

- Realize that initial start-up size is irrelevant to online Webopoly success.

- Realize that e-business competencies are very different from off-line competencies.

- Do not take on a niche competitor that has a big first-mover advantage in that niche.

- Operate through a real-time global Biznet to be super-fast in everything.

- "Clone" and extend your Biznet and brand to other products and markets.

- Develop a network of strategic partners, linked to your Biznet.

- Lease out or license your Biznet to strategic partners.

Mass-Customized Product

- Focus your Biznet on consumer "pull," not product "push."

- Optimize your search engine to allow customers to quickly find what they want, and suggest (cross-sell) complementary products or alternatives as a result.

- Help buyers make their own decisions, rather than trying to "sell" things to them.

- Allow customers to configure their own orders; offer "one-click" ordering.

- Offer limitless product selection and variety of choice.

- Be a value-added aggregator and virtual merchant of a huge product selection.

- Be a content supplier, because products are content.

Any Place + Any Time

- Leverage the Internet's exponential economies of scale and unlimited shelf space.

- Capitalize on the trend of people working from home, thus making it easier to shop online and accept doorstep deliveries.

- Perfect your logistics, thus allowing you to afford price reductions.

Dynamic Value Price

- Be the price leader and work relentlessly to cut costs and eliminate inefficiencies.

- Offer free shipping on orders above a minimal value.

- Make the smallest possible investment in inventory, zero if possible.

- Reduce working capital by collecting revenue before you need to pay suppliers.

Precise 1:1 Positioning

- Use personalization to develop long-term customer relationships.

- Use personalization to effectively make the company "My Company" to the consumer.

- Use "collaborative filtering" to "know" customers better than they know themselves.

- Surprise customers with personally appealing product offerings and suggestions.

- Focus on 1:1 precision marketing (mass marketing is irrelevant online) and turn personalization into an art form.

Personalized High-Touch Service

- Provide a personalized "Welcome" screen to the site.

- Please customers with the ease of seamless and real-time ordering.

- Surprise customers with rapid, efficient, flawless product fulfillment.

- Provide a 100 percent satisfaction guarantee, on everything you do.

Profound Brand Experience

- Place customers at the center of their own universe.

- Transform customers into their own website content.

- Get yourself onto the shopper's Favorites list or you don't count.

- Know that online brands come from reputation, which can be stored and accumulated.

- Engender word of modem to build brand reputation.

- Build a powerful brand, based on relationships and shopping experience, not products; products are no more than artifacts around which consumers have experiences; each customer has a different experience, regardless of buying products identical to those bought by other customers.

eBay
community nexus

eBay is a dynamic self-regulating
economy, where supply and demand
just balance out. Buyers attract sellers,
who in turn attract more buyers.
That's the success formula in every
product category so far.

—*Meg Whitman*
CEO, eBay

EBAY IS THE WORLD'S BIGGEST BAZAAR AND AUCTION SITE: a giant
digital trading post for practically anything. It's a Biznet, where
grandma in a nursing home can buy and sell alongside IBM.
    Motivated by a "pure, democratic vision" of a community of buy-
ers and sellers trading on equal terms, eBay was founded in 1995 (the
same year as Amazon) by Pierre Omidyar on the ethos of what a perfect market should be — where an individual was as strong as a big
corporation. Hugely profitable from the start, eBay has grown at a
meteoric pace. Net profit in 2005 will top $4 billion on a gross mer-
chandising volume of more than $40 billion.

Virtual Corporation

eBay portends a world where empowered consumers are connected in
a virtual community. Using a relatively minimal but technically
advanced Biznet infrastructure, the company handles no products; it
has no warehouses and nothing to distribute. It is an infinitely scalable, virtual Biznet Webopoly that facilitates economic transactions
between others.
    Essentially, eBay is a "context and content" intermediary — a
Biznet "medium" — that derives huge value from coordinating the
activities of more than 50 million active and enthusiastic online participants. As users flock to the eBay site, usually encouraged to go
there by word of modem, they both nourish it and feed on it. Indeed,
as discussed later, eBay's users virtually own and operate the site!
    A high-touch service provider that leverages a high-tech Internet
platform, eBay is a perfect example of the "frictionless economics"
that the Internet facilitates so well. In a virtuous cycle of wealth creation, its millions of members create a critical mass that raises huge
barriers to entry. As a result, eBay totally dominates the online person-
to-person auction market.

First-Mover Advantage

Like Amazon in online retailing, eBay was the first aggressive mover
into its e-commerce niche, and quickly leveraged that to become a
multi-service trading facilitator. Auctions did take place online pre-
eBay, as early as 1992 and before the first browser software came

along. Conducted via e-mail on text-based newsgroups and chat lists, however, they were trifling and uncoordinated efforts that could not occur in real time.

To address this opportunity, eBay opened up in 1995, first as AuctionWeb.com, and then re-engineered and re-launched its site as eBay in 1997. It quickly became so big in online auctions that it prevented Amazon from gaining any significant foothold in that e-commerce segment when it tried auctions in 1999. It also held off Yahoo, which entered the auction business in 1998. This again amply demonstrates the need to ramp up the business fast to achieve an unassailable position.

Even though both Amazon and Yahoo had a large customer base — and even though Yahoo did not charge for auction listings — both were unable to cross-sell those customers into the auction business to any meaningful degree. eBay had already made online auctions its own, at least in North America. It had sixty percent of online auction listings, compared with twenty-eight percent for Yahoo and only six percent for Amazon. By the end of 2000, eBay boasted 19 million North American registered users and was the most popular online shopping site — bigger than Amazon — with eight million items auctioned at any one time.

Then eBay branched out into the global market, extending its Biznet into both Australasia and Europe. It bought a stake in South Korea's biggest auction site, South Korea already being the world's sixth-largest Internet market. In Japan, by comparison, eBay ran into stronger competition in the form of the local Japanese firm, Rakuten, and also Yahoo, which got there just eight months ahead of eBay in a partnership with local company Softbank.

In 2002, eBay decided to pull out of Japan. In Europe, by contrast, it was Yahoo that pulled out of the online auction market in 2002, leaving it mostly to eBay, which had acquired iBazar, a leading local auction site, in 2001.

These maneuvers again show the very narrow time window in which companies can establish first-mover advantage and block new entrants, especially if they have a local partner, as eBay had in South Korea and Europe, and as Yahoo had in Japan. And as Amazon showed in general retailing, first-mover advantage clearly allows a company to establish a solid leadership position, provided it executes fast and flawlessly.

In the case of auctions, as with books or other products, sellers and buyers logically gravitate to sites where they can find most buyers and sellers. The website that quickly becomes the biggest is a magnet for future business. Again, as we see here, this phenomenon leads to natural online monopolies. And, with its Biznet now extending across all continents in tens of countries, eBay has evolved into a glocal Webopoly.

Expanding Product Range

Webopoly positions thus can be built from tiny beginnings. When eBay first started, everybody thought it was a fad, just a cute way for people to collect faddish things, or simply to get rid of junk cluttering their attics and garages. Few people thought it would last. Indeed, Pierre Omidyar first launched the auction site as a way for his girlfriend to sell Pez dispensers. Then it became the place to buy hard-to-find Beanie Babies and other collectibles like comic books and picture postcards. Within two years, however, the site was handling $2.5 million a month in transactions. Some fad!

Today, people across the world go to eBay to buy and sell all kinds of practical items, such as jewelry, cameras, computers, sporting goods, cars, and boats. There are millions of items listed on eBay across thousands of categories, from antiques and arts to time-share vacation properties and residential real estate. In effect, eBay is gradually consolidating the listing of all the items formerly found in classified advertising columns in newspapers worldwide — something the clueless newspapers should have done first, and still don't fully grasp.

Look at the huge amount of e-commerce business the newspapers have lost or missed out on. By mid-2004, eBay had 12 categories that each delivered a billion dollars or more in worldwide annual gross merchandise volume. They were the eBay Motors category (for automobiles), which handled $9.8 billion in business; five categories in the two to three billion-dollar range (Consumer Electronics, Computers, Clothing & Accessories, Books/Movies/Music, and Sports); and six categories in the one to two billion-dollar range

(Home & Garden, Collectibles, Toys, Jewelry & Watches, Cameras & Photo, and Business & Industrial).

Category Management and Marketing

eBay balances supply and demand for various products through the just-mentioned category management structure. As it grew, eBay found it necessary to manage a broad range of products. The company strategically manages its marketplace by building new and existing categories to help sellers expand sales. Category managers and teams monitor product categories and sub-categories to see whether there are too many or too few items per category, creating new categories as needed.

To generate demand, the company establishes and publishes a calendar of marketing events for the entire company. These include Internet marketing, trade shows, and print advertisements. All these methods are used to promote a certain category and to alert sellers to the upcoming opportunity. The category managers also help users enhance the presentation of their products, providing them with tools to help them buy and sell better.

Like Amazon with its zStores, eBay also has its eBay Stores feature. Buyers who shop at eBay Stores can make immediate and multiple-item purchases for both fixed-price and auctioned items. The eBay Stores feature, added in 2001, allows sellers to merchandise and brand their listings on eBay. By mid-2004, eBay was hosting more than 220,000 Stores on its website. These Webpreneurs are a growing aspect of eBay's business and they far outnumber those on the Amazon site.

Clearly, eBay differs from Amazon in several ways. These two giants differ in what, how, and to whom they sell. Amazon basically sells and ships products from itself and through third parties, as well as some through auctions and small business owners. eBay simply offers a service where others can sell through its Biznet auction site. It does not stock inventory or ship any product: the entire delivery and after-sales service cycle is handled by its members. Amazon is a retailer, eBay is not; it never lost sight of its main focus, auctions. Amazon mainly sells brand-new, brand-name, in-season retail products, with a few used books and auction items on the side. eBay services the sale of used, vintage, antique, refurbished, over-stocked, out-of-season items, with a few new and unique items on the side.

Obsessing about User Feedback

Both companies are, however, very much alike in one key business aspect. Like Amazon with its retail customers, eBay is obsessed with trying to please its users by seeing the world through their eyes. eBay CEO Meg Whitman says, "You have to honor and respond to the community of users. We are running an empowering social phenomenon."

In effect, eBay uses the Internet to tap a unique form of social capital. eBay is, as its founder hoped, a democratic community of users. They tell the world about eBay, good and bad, chatting on discussion boards to point out glitches and to lobby for changes. eBay listens intently to its users on how to improve its service so they can boost their sales, and so eBay can boost its profits in turn. The company is involved in an ongoing daily process of re-invention, even if some of the proposed changes can take months to think through and to implement.

These innovations flow from a simple but effective "Feedback Forum" rating system. Buyers and sellers rate each other, thus building a highly trustworthy trading environment where people can buy confidently from faceless strangers in far-off locales.

To buttress this self-policing community of users, the company also has an internal fraud squad in its Trust & Safety Department and uses special software to recognize typical patterns of behavior used in frauds or scams. The department patrols listings, kicks out petty offenders, and works with official law enforcement agencies to catch out-and-out crooks. As a result, eBay has surprisingly few complaints to deal with, and the rate of fraud is less than 0.01 percent — versus, for example, the credit card industry's fraud rate, which is nine times as high.

eBay also convenes "Voice of the Customer" sessions, frequently inviting new groups of sellers and buyers to head office for intense two-day dialogs. Managers grill users on issues, and users grill management on needed changes. This requires a somewhat non-traditional management style. CEO Whitman says it takes about six months for new managers to adjust to eBay's democratic regime. She says that typical business school terms like "'drive, force, commit' don't apply to us; we listen, adapt, and enable" eBay's community of users to succeed.

This community approach creates a new mode of transparent management. Executives see the flood of information that, as it spreads across the eBay Biznet, shifts power to the users and forces management to view members as collaborators. Instead of blunt bureaucratic coercion, managers must finesse their skills to provide a level of service that fosters mutual growth. Servants of the users, they succeed by leveraging the user's social capital.

Web Lifestyle Community of Webpreneurs

eBay conceptualizes its users as a community, not as customers or clients. The users are more like members who pay eBay a fee for handling their product listings.

These members also do much of eBay's work for it: they do all the product development, marketing and sales, and fulfillment. eBay supplies the Biznet platform to make it all possible. This community of users is made up of individuals, entrepreneurs, small businesses, and big corporations.

For the individuals and entrepreneurs in particular, eBay essentially becomes part of their lifestyle. Indeed, eBay has changed their lives and given them Web Lifestyles where the most active of them might be called Webpreneurs who operate online shopping businesses. In fact, hundreds of them have quit their day jobs and pursue their eBay operation as a full-time business opportunity. In turn, this has given them pride of business ownership and a hands-on understanding of how the Internet works and how economies truly function.

These users leverage eBay's Biznet to create cross-community and interpersonal relationships and to customize or personalize their online experience. Without these high-touch features, eBay might be a very fractious place that could easily get derailed by petty squabbles. But users get to know each other through the chat forums, and the more established Webpreneurs set a leadership example for others to follow. These millions of Webpreneurs suggest or make millions of small Biznet changes, and this is what optimizes the eBay market-place and keeps it stable.

To help its merchants succeed, the company also runs "eBay University" where about a thousand people come together for a day to learn marketing and sales techniques. All senior staff at eBay head-quarters also must attend these sessions at one time or another so that they get to know the users and what drives them. After the Webpreneurs return home, they apply what they learn and they frequently are able to more than double their sales quickly. As Whitman says, "If we keep listening to our users and help them grow, eBay's growth will take care of itself."

When you think about it, eBay has formed loyal partnerships with tens of millions of people, people who are launching online home-based businesses. Not all of its users are active. In mid-2004, eBay had 114 million registered users, and of that, 48 million, or 42 percent of them, were active during the most recent quarter. As well, eBay is no different from any other business in that about 20 percent of members account for about 80 percent of the transactions.

Reflecting this 80/20 rule, a new core group of eBay merchant Trading Assistants has emerged, now about 25,000 strong, who make a business out of selling for other people. Some traders are so big that eBay started a separate "PowerSellers" program to designate those who maintain who sustain monthly sales of various dollar amounts as Bronze, Silver, Gold. Platinum, or Titanium PowerSellers. They get their own logo, e-mail support, customer phone support, and even a dedicated account manager.

Investment Mistakes and Strategic Partnerships

Like Amazon, eBay made its share of investment mistakes. When you are pioneering new business models, never mind new markets and products, mistakes are inevitable. Those who never make a mistake are not innovating or breaking new ground.

One such mistake was the decision to buy brick-n-mortar auction house Butterfield & Butterfield in 1999 for $260 million. eBay thought it needed an old-fashioned auction business to legitimize its upstart online auction business. Three years later, Butterfield was irrelevant to eBay's strategy and it quit the business. But that was not before eBay formed a strategic partnership with one of the oldest and biggest names in real-world auctions, Sotheby's. Unfortunately, Sotheby's was losing money and trying to recover from a price-fixing scandal. The idea was for Sotheby's to raise eBay's profile and allow it to handle more sophisticated and higher-priced items. In the end, eBay found it could do this for itself by forging strategic partnerships with upscale and unique product companies such as Tiffany.

Much of eBay's recent growth has come from strategic partnerships with big manufacturers such as IBM and Home Depot. These big brand-name corporations bring credibility to eBay and attract yet more buyers to their product categories. Still, these companies are treated no differently from the smallest eBay trader. They get no preferential treatment in terms of product placement or exclusivity, and they are subject to the same member feedback ratings. Not all of them are being successful.

One major success, noted earlier, is the eBay Motors category, a used-car section started in 1999. Starting with unusual and antique cars, it soon became a place for mainstream listings for every kind of vehicle and even auto parts. The section then broadened out to provide end-to-end services such as auto financing, escrow, insurance, title search and registration, and inspections. By 2003, eBay was selling more automobiles than the number one US dealer, AutoNation, and this category now is by far its largest dollar volume category.

Perhaps eBay's best-ever investment and strategic partnership decision was to walk away from a $30 billion buyout offer from Yahoo in 2000. Whitman pulled out of the deal just hours before it was to be announced, because she did not want eBay to be the tag-along auction function for Yahoo's shopping portal. In hindsight that was a wise move because today eBay is trouncing Yahoo in all markets except Japan.

More recent investments focused on grabbing still more of the classified advertising market. In 2004, eBay acquired 25 percent of the local online classified ads company Craigslist.com that lists everything from apartments to used cars; 100 percent of Marketplaats, the number one classified ad website in Holland; 100 percent of Mobile in Germany; and 100 percent of Rent.com, a US apartment rental website. This thrust is part of a new "Want it Now" feature where buyers can specify exactly what they are seeking and sellers can respond to these "wants" with product information.

To pursue this expansion further, in 2005 eBay launched a new local classified ad platform called Kijiji.com (which means "village" in Swahili) as a place for international users to trade services or products that are consumed locally or which are difficult or impossible to ship around the world. Similar to the Craigslist site for U.S. users, Kijiji carries ads for babysitting services, car pooling, and casual labor, or for heavy items such as a leather ottoman or dining room furniture. This localized site further enhances eBay's glocal Biznet.

Leveraging Internet Technology

Unlike Amazon, eBay has a relatively simple Biznet model that needs no product distribution infrastructure. In fact, eBay started out as a modest auction service on Pierre Omidyar's personal home page. Even the next step was a relatively tiny investment because, as eBay expected, business growth generated enough cash flow to take care of further development costs. All eBay basically needed was a website and software clever enough to organize the listings and handle real-time, 24/7 auctions.

Initially, each bid was confirmed by e-mail and bidders were advised whenever they were outbid, thus encouraging ongoing activity. People became fascinated with the excitement of bidding and — whether buyer or seller — with the prospect of "winning." It became feverish, almost like a lottery. People found bargains, and the site did in fact grow by word of mouth.

Like Amazon, however, eBay kept adding features to the site, either of its own accord or at the behest of its members. As early as 2002, for example, based on the spread of cell phones, eBay identified wireless users as a future growth area. That same year it bought the online payment service PayPal because eBay members were already familiar with it and in fact demanded that eBay allow it to be used. So eBay simply acquired PayPal, which not only permitted easy online payments (eBay already operated its own online payment mechanism) but which also drove down back-office transaction-processing costs. As discussed later, PayPal also turned out to be a big money-making business unit.

Today, the eBay website is continually enhanced with greater levels of reliability, scalability, efficiency, and productivity. The site routinely tops website traffic rankings of unique monthly visitors. In any 24-hour period, the site can handle as many as one billion page views, one hundred million searches, and ten million bids. The site is handling almost four hundred million listings per quarter — a number that is growing by about 50 percent annually.

Like Amazon, eBay also began leasing out or licensing its Biznet platform to other big customers so that they could run eBay auctions on their own sites. In fact, eBay encouraged others to develop software that would run on top of eBay's system. This phenomenon is, in some ways, more remarkable than the Amazon situation because eBay had failed to patent its auction technology platform, thus leaving a big opening for others to enter the field. But by now it already had such a wide lead in online auctions that even this opening did not create any meaningful advantage for new entrants to enter the business.

Auction Pricing and Fee Structure

In the beginning, Omidyar did not charge anything for his simple auction service, which he promoted at no cost by listing it on various news groups to attract traffic. And today it still costs nothing for users and vendors to register at eBay.

Only when Omidyar's Internet service provider (ISP) starting billing $250 a month to host the site did the company begin charging five percent of the sales price on items going for less than $25 and 2.5 percent for more expensive items. The company became profitable in the first month and Omidyar had to hire someone to open envelopes, deposit the checks, and do the bookkeeping. Once revenue hit $10,000 in month four, he hired a manager.

All transactions were done on the traditional auction bidding model until 2001 when, to give members another option, eBay acquired the fixed-price shopping site Half.com. This division sells high-quality used books, movies, music, games, and other previously owned mass market products at about half of the original retail price — hence its name.

In 2000, eBay introduced a "But It Now" feature that lets bidders end an auction at a specified price without having to wait for the bidding to expire. This feature quickly attracted more mainstream buyers who simply don't have the time or the patience to wait for and follow the bidding process. If the price is reasonable, they just want to buy something in a fast and convenient way. Today, about 30 percent of eBay transactions are done at a fixed price.

The company charges a transaction fee on everything passing over its Biznet, including its PayPal service. PayPal has more than 50 million accounts, many of which are set up by Internet users who may never in fact use eBay. PayPal is an ideal solution for individual, small, and perhaps some mid-sized merchants who may be unable to get a brand-name credit card merchant account. As an online payment mechanism, PayPal also facilitates the settlement of cross-border transactions as eBay grows in global markets.

Glocal (Global + Local) Multi-Channel Expansion

eBay's business began, of course, in the United States. But eBay has adapted itself to both local domestic and global national markets; it has developed a glocal marketplace. In the United States, eBay has scores of localized websites where users can more easily find and browse for items in their local geographic area. In each of its global markets, eBay operates country-specific sites, thus adapting its presentation, and tailoring its content, to the needs of local customers.

Whitman claims that eBay knows "more about managing a marketplace than anyone else in the world." This glocal approach certainly is generating rapid expansion and record profitability. The company is taking business away from online and offline competitors, and its business outside North America is booming. None of this expansion would be possible without its three-dimensional Biznet.

As well as expanding globally, in the US eBay now has hundreds of independent local third-party "drop-off" stores, taking eBay implicitly into a multi-channel retailing world. However, these drop-off stores were set up by eBay re-sellers — the Trading Assistants mentioned earlier — to cater to sellers who don't want to handle the complexity and hassles of online fulfillment. This gives eBay a brick-n-mortar presence without having to invest a cent in real estate or pay rent.

The company also launched a magazine-size, 32-page catalog for the US year-end 2004 holiday shopping season. Millions of copies were mailed out and, if the catalog is considered a success, eBay says it will consider publishing more catalogs periodically. While items are listed with photos and an average selling price, they must be bought online. This step again begins to give eBay some multi-channel characteristics.

Conclusions and Outlook for eBay

In its first full year, 1996, eBay reported a profit of $3.3 million, but that was just the beginning. Gross profit in 2004 reached $3.3 billion and eBay expects that to zoom to $4.2 billion in 2005. The company's gross profit margin is more than 80 percent, its operating profit margin is close to 35 percent, and net income is about 25 percent of sales. These juicy profit margins are far higher than any other e-commerce company — indeed, higher than most businesses of any kind — and are due to the scalability of eBay's relatively simple, low-cost Biznet model.

Can eBay sustain these margins and this kind of growth?

Well, if eBay is a fad, it is a pretty big fad. You might think that at some point the company is going to exhaust the available supply of readily tradable merchandise as more and more consumers empty their closets.

On the other hand, we live in a highly materialistic society where people seem to have an insatiable appetite for consumer goods, many of which they do not need and rarely if ever use. And huge populations in developing countries are moving into the middle class and have a tendency to copy the acquisitive consumption habits of the West. For the foreseeable future, there seems to be more than enough supply and demand to maintain eBay's exponential growth.

There might be business fluctuations depending on the strength of the overall economy. And, as its business matures, eBay might be counter-cyclical. For example, in tougher economic times, shoppers may be more inclined to search eBay for bargains or to use eBay to turn surplus household items into cash. In better economic times, there may be fewer bargain hunters and fewer people anxious to unload stuff. On the other hand, people might spend more on collectibles (an eBay specialty) at these times.

But evidence of such cycles has not yet shown up in eBay's growth path, despite disasters like 9/11 and other economic disruptions due to the conflicts in the Middle East. The business has grown smoothly and strongly. And if eBay continues to pull other partners aboard its Biznet platform, that should earn large revenues.

In sum, eBay quickly tapped into a pent-up demand for a simple way to trade in used products. It leveraged the network effects of the Internet to bring together global intermediaries in a giant Biznet that can handle complex, unique, high-value items as well as simple, practical, low-value items. The company achieved a leadership position and widespread brand recognition, quickly getting itself placed on Web surfers' Favorites lists as the best place to easily buy and sell used merchandise. As the biggest such facilitator, it simply pulled more and more buyers and sellers into its Biznet orbit.

The company also demonstrates how to build a virtual business where intangible assets can be worth billions. It built and leveraged a global brand, a glocal market penetration, and a secure Biznet platform. Then it merged this with the immense social capital of its users to create huge shareholder value. The company took a brilliant idea and, through careful management execution, monitoring, and constant innovation, turned it into a gold mine. eBay is not just a wildly successful dot-com startup; it invented a whole new way of doing business.

Strategy Lessons from eBay about Biznets and the "6 Ps" of Biznet Marketing

Biznet
- Realize that initial start-up size is irrelevant to online Webopoly success.

- Create your Biznet as an economically elastic network of individual Webpreneurs.

- Rapidly scale up a meta-mediary Biznet of solo Webpreneurs (nano-businesses) to create a global growth phenomenon and ultimately a Webopoly.

- Build a scalable Biznet to handle all content, transactions, and user feedback.

- Quickly build a critical mass of loyal customers to raise huge barriers to entry.

- Expand rapidly into other markets, if need be with a local partner.

- License your Biznet to other companies.

Mass-Customized Product

- Be a content-based infomediary; handle no products.

- Optimize your search engine to allow customers to quickly find what they want.

- Practice category management and marketing.

- Use segment-targeted catalogs to engender transactions, build categories.

- Establish and follow a strategic marketing calendar, managing it online.

- Form strategic partnerships with big product vendors.

- Build your brand on relationships and the shopping experience, not products.

Any Place + Any Time

- Build an online agora or bazaar-based Biznet to allow solo Webpreneurs to participate, regardless of location.

- Capitalize on the social trend of people working from home and also provide them with a home-based business opportunity.

- Be a glocal company and tailor everything to local markets.

- Provide click-and-mortar product "pick-up/drop-off" facilities.

Dynamic Value Price

- Offer free memberships but charge fees on every product processed over your Biznet.

- Offer a choice of pricing: auctions or fixed-price.

- Minimize invested capital per unit of revenue and profit.

Precise 1:1 Positioning

- Focus on 1:1 personalized high-touch service to entrepreneurial users/customers or self-employed Webpreneurs.

- Tap the potential of Webpreneurs, who understand the e-commerce dynamics of life because they are starting to live a Web Lifestyle.

- Become part of the customer's lifestyle, the Web Lifestyle.

Personalized High-Touch Service

- Leverage all your intangible assets.

- Incorporate human values in your business strategies.

- Tap into and leverage the "social capital" of your user base.

- Invest heavily in user/customer education and knowledge to boost growth.

Profound Brand Experience

- See the world through the customer's eyes.

- Obsess over customer/user feedback; adapt your Biznet to further enable customers.

- Empower customers/users by providing a virtual community so that they can interact.

- Recognize that virtual network democracies easily beat big bureaucratic firms.

- Build brand loyalty by realizing that community-based members have a high investment in both time and emotion spent on your Biznet.

- Cement customer relationships through a sense of community.
- Engender word of modem feedback to build brand equity and trust.
- Get your website onto the user's Favorites list or you don't exist.

Dell
mass customizer

**E-Commerce is the most efficient
transaction medium we can think of —
apart from mental telepathy. We
acquire our competitors one customer
at a time.**

*—Michael Dell
founder and Chairman, Dell*

STARTING WITH ONE COMPUTER BUILT IN MICHAEL DELL'S
university dorm in 1983, Dell now is the number one PC manufacturer on the planet. Dell custom-builds PCs based on exactly those
components and features requested by individual online buyers.

Dell pioneered a new business model focused on phenomenal
speed: lightning-fast, mass-customized execution of online orders
and direct shipment. This eliminates costly middleman retailers and
allows Dell to offer lower prices. By creating tightly linked partnerships with component suppliers and service providers — by creating
a Biznet — Dell makes customers feel they are dealing with one large
but super-efficient company that treats their unique needs individually and personally.

The result: while competitors who sell through retail channels
struggle, Dell's net profit is almost a billion dollars per quarter and is
growing at a 25 percent annual clip, on annual sales nearing $50 bil-
lion. Dell came from nowhere to dominate the global PC market.

First-Mover "Direct" Sales Advantage

Twenty years ago, any alert college freshman could have bought the
necessary components and, in his spare time, assembled a PC just as
well but more cheaply than any PC manufacturing company.
Michael Dell was one who used that advantage in 1983 to start selling PCs with his name on them, directly to customers via small ads
in trade magazines, at a 15 percent discount to established brands.
He was so successful that within a year he had to drop out of college
to attend to his growing business. He was doing six million dollars in
volume by then, and seventy million dollars by the end of 1985. This
was all by mail-order; the Internet wasn't yet available to him.

By 1990, other low-overhead mail-order firms began to imitate
Dell's approach, threatening to undercut his prices. Then Dell made a
strategic error in 1991 by trying to sell indirectly through electronics
retailers. This did boost sales but it also caught Dell in a cash crunch
and in 1993 the company lost money, primarily because it lost the ability to customize the orders. By mid-1994, Dell wisely abandoned the
retail chains to focus 100 percent on its "Dell direct" model.

In 1995, stressing the importance of early Internet leadership,
Dell designed its first Web storefront. Michael Dell told his website

designers, "It's more valuable to be in front with an imperfect site than a late-comer with a perfect site." The site was launched in mid-1996 and by year-end was selling one million dollars a day.

Thanks to the maturing of e-commerce on the Internet, sales jumped 49 percent per year on average from 1994 to 1999, with profits soaring 62 percent annually to reach $1.7 billion. In 1999 Dell became the number one PC maker in the United States, with a 16 percent market share. Today, it has about 33 percent (and growing) of the US market and is ranked number one in the world with 17 percent of the market, compared with 15 percent for Hewlett-Packard (which absorbed Compaq), and only six percent for IBM.

Dell's online selling model took full advantage of the fact that the PC fundamentally changed the structure of the computer industry. Previously, the industry consisted of clunky, vertically integrated companies such as IBM, DEC, and NCR. They developed their own components, built them into mainframe computers, and ran them with their own software.

The personal computer flattened the industry into a networked horizontal structure — an industry-wide Biznet — with key players such as Intel and Microsoft supplying the components and the software. Companies such as Compaq and Hewlett Packard started to mass-produce IBM-PC "clones" and sell them through retail channels. Dell saw how he could out-compete them by selling customized PCs directly to the buyer. Today, built-to-order PC by built-to-order PC, customer by customer, Dell is putting all its competitors out of business.

Indeed, having essentially launched the global PC industry, IBM announced in 2004 that it was abandoning the PC business entirely and sold that operation to the leading Chinese computer manufacturer, Lenovo. Dell said it had no interest in buying the business because it even out-competes Lenovo on its own turf, in China, forcing it to cut prices there.

Dell's "3D-Glocal" Biznet

Today's PCs are becoming something of a commodity, but Dell profitably leverages the network economics of connecting suppliers to customers via a Biznet. Dell's model smashes the traditional value chain and reconfigures it into a value "web." To best serve customers, Dell's Biznet closely links a variety of component suppliers, systems integrators, original equipment manufacturers, hardware and software providers, service support and repair companies, and logistics companies.

And because Dell aligns its marketing and service operations to suit local market conditions (that is, Dell is a glocal company), Dell created distinct sub-Biznets in each geographic region and sub-sub-Biznets on a national basis. In other words, Dell's Biznet operates in 3D.

Dell has more than 80 websites tailored to the needs of particular countries or regions, offering local-language websites that also are attuned to local cultures and business norms. It also customizes its products for different markets, with localized keyboards and local-language software and documentation.

Dell also decides where to locate its facilities based on an obsessive drive to minimize costs while still being able to build to order products of the highest value, and to sell them direct on a global basis. Dell is the only company still assembling PCs in the USA. But there, as across the world, it deliberately avoids high-cost areas where electronics manufacturers have already clustered. Rather, it goes to strategically logistical low-cost locations and thus attracts suppliers to also set up there, alongside Dell assembly plants, so that it can assemble in real time.

Real-Time Manufacturing

Dell products literally come into its plants through one door as disparate components and, within minutes, go out of another door as ready-to-use PCs in shipping cartons.

Dell suppliers keep components warehoused within minutes of Dell's factories. Suppliers are told exactly what daily production requirements are, based on new online orders Dell has received. In some cases, components are actually kept in dozens of trucks backed up to receiving docks, and are pulled off as needed onto the assembly line. Should a single truck be a few minutes late, a production line will stop, so tight is the scheduling.

Whether the components are already at the receiving dock or due to arrive in minutes, supplier personnel are located inside Dell's plants where they call for new material from their warehouses and trucks using Dell's Biznet. The supplier thus not only manages the materials flow but holds the inventory on its books until the moment a component actually goes into a computer.

In fact, through its Biznet, Dell reschedules every assembly line around the world every two hours. It brings into the factory only two hours' worth of materials. Each factory runs with only five to six hours' worth of inventory, including work in process.

These hyper-efficient plants are equipped with triple-decker conveyor belts that bring bins filled with parts. They lower the parts mechanically and automatically to precisely the one assembler (on a team in the hundreds) who configures the PC exactly as one specific customer ordered it. Completed PCs go by conveyor belt to the shipping area where they are boxed by robots and then routed to yet more dozens of idling trucks, all ready to depart as soon as they are loaded, which takes less than 30 minutes.

A typical Dell assembly plant turns out a minimum of 50,000 computers a day. An order that hits the factory floor at nine A.M. is out of the door and motoring down the highway in a delivery truck by no later than one P.M. This dazzling efficiency has left Dell, as just noted, as the only company still assembling PCs in the USA. While others were forced to move offshore, Dell operates three giant assembly plants in the USA and is building two more, each as big as six contiguous football fields.

Driving Costs Down

In 1999, it took two Dell workers 14 minutes to assemble a PC; now a single worker does it in only five minutes. Thanks to re-arrangements in warehouse flows and elimination of needless assembly steps, the cost of assembly dropped and worker efficiency climbed. Even though pneumatic screwdrivers are used, eliminating even a single screw from a product saves four seconds per machine. Applying one less sticker per machine saves more seconds. The desire to be low-cost leader drives Dell to eliminate pennies while maintaining quality.

Dell also monitors its assembly line workers closely and trains them to achieve high levels of performance. The most expert assemblers are designated as "master builders" and videotaped so that others may watch and learn how it should be done. They work in teams and are set what might seem like irrational goals, such as a 30 percent increase in output. But these stretch goals end up achieving a 15 percent gain that otherwise would not have occurred because the large goal forces the team to think in non-conventional ways about how to improve.

As a result of its fanatical focus on efficiency, the labor cost of an average Dell computer is only $10, or less than two percent of Dell's gross product cost per PC. Dell also spends two percent of net profits on research and development. This is not spent on developing new products *per se* — that's up to the suppliers — but rather on innovating how Dell assembles and packages a built-to-order product.

However, in terms of new products, thanks to its real-time assembly process Dell also can always make available the most advanced computers. For example, as soon as a new chip is released, Dell can start using it almost immediately, while competitors have to work off their existing inventory.

Real-time assembly also means Dell can fix any mistakes very quickly and precisely. When Intel once produced a faulty Pentium chip, Dell knew how many computers had that chip, exactly where they were, and was able to replace the chip right away. Manufacturers working through retail distribution channels didn't have a clue which PCs had the faulty chips. They had to stop their production lines until a new supply of chips arrived and had to hunt down the faulty PCs. Dell just kept on assembling with brand new chips and sent out new chips to replace the faulty ones.

Dell thus is always first to market with the latest and most reliable PC and can cut prices without hurting profit margins. It readily kills off commoditized products as they become obsolete and leaps to the next generation of computers, thus maintaining value leadership and margins.

Cash-Flow Benefits

Real-time customer ordering and manufacturing have huge financial benefits for Dell. As noted, suppliers are required to account for inventory until the moment it not only enters the plant, including any components sitting in trucks at receiving docks, but until it goes into a computer. In effect, then, Dell holds zero components in inventory.

Dell also requires its suppliers to repeatedly reduce component prices. In return, Dell rewards the suppliers with bigger orders and long-term contract commitments. In turn, this pressures component suppliers to become more efficient and innovative.

In bypassing intermediaries, Dell significantly reduces its channel costs from around fifteen percent of sales to only two percent of sales. And, like Amazon, Dell also gets paid by its customers before it has to pay suppliers for components. Buyers typically pay by credit card and, while the payment is authorized right away, the card is only charged upon delivery. Even including corporate clients that buy with purchase orders, Dell's accounts receivable are collected at least two weeks prior to Dell having to pay suppliers. This gives Dell two weeks' free supply of cash on all its sales transactions. This so-called "negative cash conversion rate" is a huge financial positive: it significantly minimizes Dell's working capital needs.

Product Range Expansion and Cross-Selling

Dell quickly expanded its 1985 product offerings from IBM-compatible desktop PCs to laptops in 1987. Later it added all kinds of software, printers, and other peripherals. Dell's website did not readily support "cross-category shopping" from its desktop, laptop, server, and printer product listings. But it did begin to put its own brand name on printers and projectors, and launched its own servers and handhelds. More recent additions to the product line were digital cameras and Dell big-screen TVs. At this point, in 2003, Dell realized it needed to completely redesign its website to support a multi-category shopping experience.

These consumer electronics items were a natural extension of Dell's product portfolio and gave customers a single source for their consumer technology needs. In fact, Dell now uses its website to cross-sell this product range to customers as they are configuring their PCs online, suggesting product additions and even throwing in free upgrades on screens and software, or free printers and cameras, plus free shipping, as incentives for taking a specific computer model configuration.

This diversification is paying off handsomely. After entering the printer market with its own brand in 2004, within nine months Dell had captured a 13 percent market share. Also in 2004, Dell embarked on a strategy of drawing customers to its wider offering of consumer products. The goal is to make its PC the center of digital in-home entertainment set-ups. To this end, Dell is pushing its own "media experience" software over Microsoft's Windows XP Media Edition software.

Dell's Biznet also uses customer relationship management (CRM) software to record all interactions with its 30 million-plus unique customers so that it knows exactly who they are. It thus has a large amount of information it can draw upon to target customers for repeat and expanded sales, or to cross-sell additional products and services. It can determine purchasing behavior, anticipate demand levels for various products, and measure customer satisfaction levels. By anticipating demand, Dell assesses replacement cycles in different markets and different customer segments, and can thus target customers either online, through catalog mailings, or with a direct sales force.

To better serve customers, Dell's website mirrors its customer segmentation strategy, with pages for home and home office users, small business, medium and large business, government, education, and healthcare sector clients. The website also has weekly specials and there usually is a brand-new product offering each week — so fast is the pace of change in the industry on which Dell immediately capitalizes.

Strategic Marketing and Customer Segmentation

Dell is very much market-focused, with about one-third of its employees in sales and marketing. Country managers and sales reps are credited with sales on their customer accounts, whether the purchase was made online, over the phone, or in person. Managers and sales reps are rewarded based on the gross margin of the sale, thus encouraging them to up-sell and cross-sell the customer into high-margin products.

Dell classifies its customers into two basic segments:

1. transactional customers (mainly individuals and small businesses) who buy one or two PCs online as a consumer purchase and pay for them immediately; and

2. relationship customers (larger corporate and public sector accounts) who treat PCs as capital investments and buy or lease multiple PCs with purchase orders.

Dell's 30-million-plus-customer CRM database is 30 percent transactional, 40 percent relationship, and 30 percent a mixture of the two.

Relationship customer accounts are initially secured by local sales reps and serviced by a dedicated support team. Small businesses and retail buyers are served either online or by phone reps who use pull up historical sales profiles through the CRM software to help customers make buying decisions that best suit their prior purchases.

For larger customers, who are less price-sensitive, Dell tends to focus on PCs with more advanced features and bigger price tags. This also applies to the transactional customer, where Dell tends to target the more literate computer user rather than first-time buyers who are more price-sensitive.

To provide sharper focus on customer needs, Dell further segments the market into finer slices so that it can better tailor products to individual needs. The largest corporate accounts are designated as "platinum" or "gold" based on their purchase volume.

Dell also holds forums with these groups where, through dialog, close interaction, and careful listening, Dell gains feedback on their evolving needs. Michael Dell himself even hangs out in Internet chat rooms to see what Dell users are saying about their purchases. As Dell observes, "It's all about shrinking the time and resources required to meet customer needs in a world where those needs are constantly changing."

Premium Attention to "Premier" Customers

Dell's largest clients have their own dedicated "Premier" Web pages that they log into at Dell and can customize to their own needs. All Premier pages are customized for each Premier customer, with user names and passwords for authorized personnel. Dell's sales teams like to wow potential customers by building a customized Premier extranet for them, just to show the Biznet functionality they will enjoy by picking Dell as their supplier.

The pages include asset management, software upgrades, technical support, and procurement capabilities. Premier pages also marshal a slew of customized information. These include detailed purchase history reports, standard configurations for different corporate departments or functions, and paperless online purchase order capability.

Large customer pages are further customized to link their own internal procurement systems to Dell's Biznet so that orders flow directly to its order management system. Dell also helps Premier customers plan their PC replacement and upgrade cycles. Indeed, many big customers outsource their PC procurement to Dell, which manages their PC inventory, from purchase to disposition, and also helps them dispose of used equipment.

One-to-One Customer Focus

Dell believes in "creating loyal customers by providing a superior experience" at a greater value than the competition. As Dell claims on its website, "We do business directly with customers, one at a time, and believe we do it better than anyone on the planet." Amazon might justifiably take issue with that, but Dell surely is best at online computer sales and service.

Every system Dell assembles already has a waiting customer. The Dell Direct model starts and ends with the customer, using direct relationships to drive the customer experience. It provides the most efficient path to the customer, with a single point of accountability, making Dell the low-cost, build-to-order provider of standards-based computers and related technology. It customizes each buyer's choice of high-quality, latest-technology, high-value systems and backs it up with superior client-tailored service and support.

A major key to Dell's online success is customer choice, convenience, and control. The site lets buyers "virtually assemble" their PC, component by component, feature by feature, reconfiguring it as they go along, updating features and prices to suit their needs and their budget.

Online service tools, available to all customers, including Premier customers, are several. They include the ability to track your order status, a Dell knowledge base of product information and frequently asked questions (FAQs), plus a file library of downloadable drivers, utilities, and other updates. Dell also operates its own online bulletin board where buyers can ask questions and share ideas, either with each other or with technical experts.

If need be, customers can place their tentative order "on hold" in their online shopping cart and then call up Dell customer service to ensure that what they've ordered is truly going to meet their needs. The Dell service rep can open that customer's shopping cart and review the transaction with the customer, over the phone or with live online voice or e-mail chat. This high-touch approach solidifies the customer relationships and ensures a much deeper degree of customer satisfaction with the product they eventually buy.

In case problems do arise after product delivery, Dell PCs come preloaded with Dell's "Resolution Assistant" software. It can gather information from the PC and send it to Dell technicians so that they can work with the customer to troubleshoot the problem. An executable software module to solve the problem can usually be sent back to the PC to fix it automatically. This support system cuts the number of physical service calls by 90 percent, slashing Dell's service costs appreciably.

Strategic Customer Service Partnerships

Dell works closely with numerous partners, all linked through its Biznet, to satisfy customer needs and expectations and to make its business model effective. As we've seen, these include a cluster of component suppliers, peripheral manufacturers, and software providers.

Dell also has another cluster of post-purchase installers, system integrators, service providers, consultants, and on-site repair partners, especially for its largest customers. These service partners include, perhaps surprisingly, companies such as IBM that, had it adapted faster, should have dominated the PC market Dell now commands.

These service partners typically are located close to the customer and handle about 10 percent of service calls. Other service calls, as just described, are usually handled online or over the phone through service support call centers.

Dell clearly makes extensive use of outsourcing. But it says it will never outsource its build-to-order final assembly operations because that is the company's secret "black box." It is so proprietary and strategic to the company's competitive advantage that it is afraid of losing those competencies to sub-contractors.

Otherwise, information flows freely back and forth between Dell, its customers, and its strategic partners across its Biznet. Orders are captured, supplies are triggered, assembly is completed, products are shipped, and service is attended to in rapid-fire sequence. Through its Biznet, Dell melds the capabilities of its partners into a distinct and so far unbeatable competitive advantage.

Conclusions and Outlook for Dell

Dell's leadership position flows from early Internet exploitation and a fierce commitment to offer the highest-quality, custom-built, latest-feature computers on the market. Dell's real-time Biznet allows it to solidify and control, if not own, its customer relationships.

Market domination depends on thinking ahead, making fast decisions, and sustaining high speed. Dell sustains speed by a relentless focus on operational excellence and customer satisfaction. Its customer feedback system and Biznet linkages with suppliers enable it to anticipate future market needs, spot trends early, and get its hands on the latest components the moment they become available.

Dell solidifies its leadership position through product and service reliability. Its products are second to none in quality and reliability, right from the moment you lift them out of the shipping carton and boot them up for the first time. Dell's brand quality has built loyal long-term customers: users typically come back again and again for the latest product once they decide it's time to upgrade.

Dell orchestrates the entire value-building process and reaps rich rewards for its pioneering e-commerce efforts. The company achieves superior performance in inventory turnover, reduced overhead, cash conversion, return on investment, shareholder return, and customer satisfaction. It overtook all its outmoded competitors and is leaving them behind.

This outstanding success comes against a backdrop of declining PC prices (driven by Dell itself!) that caused other PC makers to falter and report huge losses. Dell did not so much survive this environment as create it and mold it to its own profitable advantage. Its direct model drives prices down while keeping quality high, thus enabling it to vanquish competitors who stick with the old way of doing things. It is the PC industry's Biznet Webopoly.

Strategy Lessons from Dell about Biznets and the "6 Ps" of Biznet Marketing

Biznet

- Gain first-mover advantage by differentiating your Biznet model as "direct."

- Launch a horizontal Biznet to take advantage of the inefficient vertical industry model.

- Focus on phenomenal speed, with lightning-fast assembly.

- Quickly build a critical mass of loyal customers.

- Form strategic partnerships with suppliers.

- "Clone" and extend your Biznet to other products and markets.

Mass-Customized Product

- Let each customer "build to order" their product online; assemble it and ship it direct.

- Allow the customer to build to order, thus reducing product development costs by identifying, in real-time, what the marketplace really wants.

- Give every customer full choice, convenience, and control over their order process.

- Always be first to market with the very latest technology.

- Build a powerful brand based on high-quality, latest-features products.

- Kill off commoditized products as soon as they become obsolete.

- Move from "just-in-time" to "real-time" assembly.
- Identify "master builders" among assembler workforce.
- Teach others how to be master builders.
- Broaden out your product range and cross-sell the customer to other categories.

Any Place + Any Time

- Be a glocal company, tailoring everything to local market conditions.
- Have fleets of idling trucks at both the receiving and shipping docks.
- Capitalize on the Web Lifestyle trend of people working from home, thus making it easier to shop online and accept doorstep deliveries.
- Realize that the need to "touch and feel" electronics products is low, as is their rate of return, thus making brick-n-mortar retailing for such products obsolete.

Dynamic Value Price

- Be the low-cost leader of high-quality, latest-technology products.
- Ensure customers feel they are getting the lowest price available for a leading brand.
- Offer free upgrades and free shipping on all orders.
- Reward sales reps based on the gross margin of products, not their total sales value.
- Transform your capital and cost structures, minimizing invested capital per unit of revenue and profit.
- Build assembly plants in low-cost areas, attract suppliers to locate near you, not vice versa.
- Establish a "negative-cash conversion rate" by getting paid for products before you pay suppliers.

- Perfect your logistics, thus allowing you to afford price reductions.

- Focus obsessively on driving down costs; hold zero or minimum inventory.

- Fix any mistakes fast and with exacting precision.

Precise 1:1 Positioning

- Use your Biznet to build a database of all customers.

- Determine customer purchase behavior to anticipate and forecast demand.

- Segment and sub-segment customers into groups and structure your website and ordering accordingly; target segments for repeat and expanded sales; separate transactional from higher-value relationship customers.

- Replace one-size-fits-all websites with customized sites for customers and partners; give "Premier" customers their own "Premier" website linked to your Biznet, and assign dedicated sales reps to them.

- Use 1:1 relationships to drive the customer experience; take customer personalization to an art form to permit 1:1 precision marketing.

- Cultivate long-term customer relationships.

Personalized High-Touch Service

- Solve as many customer problems online or over the Internet as possible.

- Digitize the problem-solution process via downloadable information and/or software that will "fix" the problem automatically.

- Form strategic service partnerships to "outsource" customer service on a seamless basis.

Profound Brand Experience

- Use a Biznet to lower the cost of product innovation and customization, boosting buyer satisfaction and product demand.

- Be the single-source supplier to your customers for all related needs.

- Provide special forums for "Premier" customers to obtain their feedback.

- Operate a bulletin board to obtain feedback and answer customer queries.

- Measure customer satisfaction levels.

Quixtar
webpreneur
franchise

We're successful because we're different. We combine the Internet with the individual, through independent business ownership and person-to-person contact.

—*Doug DeVos, President*
Quixtar Inc.

QUIXTAR IS A PHENOMENAL DOT-COM SUCCESS, profitable from day one. The affiliate marketing company's independent business owners (IBOs) earn commission income based on the sales they generate through a four-part "I-Commerce" model: Internet, Individuals, Infrastructure (Quixtar's product distribution platform, or Biznet), and Independent business ownership.

This model lets Webpreneurs own a turnkey Web-based business without the expense of a website of their own, or any product development or distribution hassles. Product marketing and ordering is done online, via the Quixtar website and a replenishment ordering system called "Ditto" delivery, where the shopper "pulls" the product through the system. Business development is done in person, on a one-to-one basis, but with team support and training. The company does not advertise, but already is doing one billion dollars in annual sales and returning huge profits to its IBOs.

Fast-Paced, Record-Breaking Start-Up

Quixtar was late to the Webolution, launching its site in late 1999, just six months before the dot-com bubble burst. But when it showed up, it made a grand entrance — launching with an overnight "Big Bang" total-system conversion — and never looked back.

Within two weeks, Quixtar was the fifth-ranked global shopping site, logging 52 million page views and racking up its first one-million-dollar sales day. Within one hundred days, sales topped one hundred million dollars, with daily sales averaging two million dollars. After two hundred days, sales topped $250 million, and it wasn't long before Quixtar kept recording new peak sales days and, in late 2004, it racked up a $12 million sales day.

In its first full year online (2000), Quixtar sold $518 million worth of merchandise versus only $147 million by Amazon in its first year, and only $32 million by eBay in its start-up year. In 2001, Quixtar sales leaped to $816 million — remarkable amid a dot-com shakeout, a stock market meltdown, an economic slowdown, and 9/11 — and climbed further to $958 million in 2002. Sales surged past the billion-dollar mark in 2003 and climbed just as strongly through 2004.

Quixtar thus quickly became a big winner, one of the Internet's top e-commerce businesses. In September 2000, on Quixtar's first anniversary online, the National Retail Federation's *Stores* magazine ranked Quixtar seventh among e-commerce websites. The climb up the website rankings didn't stop there. A study by Deloitte & Touche, the big global audit firm, ranked Quixtar the number two retail website in Canada, topped only by Sears (the subject of this book's next chapter).

Then, in 2001, *Business 2.0* magazine ranked Quixtar number one in the health and beauty category — a lead it maintains today and has built upon — and Harris Interactive later estimated Quixtar had 22 percent of all online sales in that category, way ahead of its lagging competitors Avon, Mary Kay, and Herbalife. In 2004, for example, Avon suffered a nine percent drop in US operating profit as it grappled with weaker sales of key beauty items, due largely, in my opinion, to Quixtar's successful online expansion.

Later in 2001, *Inter@ctive Week* magazine ranked Quixtar as second only to Amazon (and way ahead of eBay) in overall online retail sales. In 2004, some rankings showed Quixtar in 12th place in global rankings. But some of the names ahead of it were companies such as eBay and Dell, which log many business-to-business sales and many big-ticket items such as cars and computers. Almost all of Quixtar's sales are small-ticket personal and household replenishment items purchased by individuals.

Highly Effective Website for Consumers and IBOs

When launched, Quixtar's website was as big as that of General Motors. During the first 24 hours, the site was overwhelmed by 20 million hits from people wanting to shop there.

Still, the initial website did suffer from a few design and usability problems. Quixtar got away with these shortcomings for a while because its committed IBOs were going to shop through the site, no matter how cumbersome it was. But the new tech-savvy IBO that Quixtar wanted to attract found the site lacking. It was organized more to reflect how Quixtar operates than how people actually shop online. Such a design flaw is not uncommon. Wal-Mart's first website had the look and feel of its brick-n-mortar stores, leading to its mediocre performance.

The Quixtar site was overhauled throughout 2003 and re-launched with a brand new look in 2004. It has vastly improved navigation and functionality, and more prominent product displays. As well, a French-language site was launched for users in bilingual Canada, plus a site in Spanish (Quixtar Para Ti) for Hispanic populations in the United States and Puerto Rico.

The new site is a personalized shopping portal that is functional, fun, and easy to use. It is clean and zesty, with lots of lifestyle appeal for the modern consumer. It appeals to young consumers because it doesn't so much sell products as a new lifestyle — a Web Lifestyle — and a way for people to start a Web-based business. Quixtar thus does now reach tech-savvy, independent-minded people who want to both shop at home and participate in the e-commerce Webolution through private business ownership.

When you visit the Quixtar site or, more likely, are referred there by an existing IBO, you can elect to participate on one of three levels: as a client, as a member, or as an IBO yourself. Clients are regular online shoppers who enjoy the product offerings and the time-saving convenience and experience of shopping online to get products delivered. For a nominal annual $20 fee, members get extra savings through discount pricing and membership perks, somewhat like a shopping club but with the added benefits again of online shopping and home delivery.

However, most Quixtar participants realize that to be a commission-earning IBO is by far the best option. If you appreciate the benefits of shopping online, why not build your own online business with Quixtar in the process? As mentioned, IBO shoppers earn a commission on everything they buy through their own Quixtar business, as well as on all purchases by people the IBO introduces to the business. This model is offered only by affiliate marketing companies, of which Quixtar is the leader.

"Ditto" Delivery to the Doorstep

For generations, even before supermarkets came along, people have been in the habit of writing out almost the same weekly shopping list. Most of the items on that list are replenishment products we purchase over and over again, week in, week out. Then we trudge off to spend two hours in a supermarket or warehouse club, gathering up hefty items, almost walking the aisles blindfolded to pick them off the same shelf as last week, and then lugging them all home.

Those grocery days are now coming to an end (as shown by the Tesco online supermarket case, later in this book). Thanks to the Webolution of shopping, we can order not just replenishment items but any product online by simply checking off boxes on an automatic re-order list and then have it all delivered. And Quixtar's "Ditto" delivery system allows shoppers and IBOs to do just that.

Ditto delivery is a simple process that, once you get it set up for the first order, operates virtually automatically. The system first lets you analyze your household needs. Then you compile a standing order Ditto delivery list that, of course, you can vary at any time later to suit your changing product or budgetary needs. You zap off your order as and when needed, and simply sit back and wait for the goods to arrive on your doorstep.

Successful IBOs Earn a Large Business Income

The Ditto delivery system also allows Quixtar IBOs to track the Point Value (PV) of the purchases they make, and also the PV of orders submitted by clients, members, or IBOs they have personally registered into their business. The system tracks PV automatically and forecasts it out into the future. IBOs know exactly how much commission they will earn this month and in future months, based on all the submitted Ditto orders by each and every client, member, and IBO on their team or IBO organization.

The bigger the sales volume, the higher the PV, and the fatter the IBO's profit. The performance bonus ranges from a lowly three percent (on an easily achieved 100 PV) up to twenty-five percent on a monthly PV of 7,500-plus for the IBO's business group. IBOs with even a small organization thus effectively get their own products paid for, and then some, by the commissions they earn.

IBOs reach progressively higher levels of success and commission rates as they build their business organization. The average net business income of an IBO at the Emerald level, for example, is around US$60,000 per year. Those at Diamond level and above all pull in six-figure annual net profits, some of them approaching a million dollars. The company's compensation plan also pays special incentive bonuses to IBOs who build and sustain large business groups.

The ability to forecast PV and set PV targets thus is a key incentive for IBOs in driving and managing the growth of their Quixtar business. The commissions and incentive bonuses paid out to IBOs by Quixtar in 2004 was almost $400 million. This profit distribution clearly shows the benefits of this type of business ownership as a product marketing strategy.

Sales growth also sets in motion a virtuous cycle of revenue generation. As sales and PV grow so do corporate and IBO profits, in turn encouraging IBOs to move up the commission bracket ladder to earn still more. As the online consumer base expands — and assuming IBOs become more experienced in their business development and marketing efforts (discussed later) — IBOs and Quixtar have the potential to achieve exponential growth, with little or no increase in costs.

Ideal e-Shopping Product Range

Another major factor in Quixtar's rapid growth and its future potential is its wide selection (some 13,000 product types) of non-perishable, replacement-item household and personal consumables that are perfect for the online retail world. Examples are cleaning products, skin care and cosmetics items, and vitamins and wellness products — just the kinds of things people buy repeatedly and that are easy to ship to the home.

No list of products can do justice to everything Quixtar has available, which is virtually anything a family might ever need. To begin with, the website offers Quixtar's own exclusive brands in three main sections: Home, Health, and Personal Care.

Home products encompass a whole range of laundry, furniture, floor, kitchen, bathroom, auto, and multi-purpose cleaners and polishes, with SA8 laundry products being the best-known Quixtar brand in this group. Health products are the well-known Nutrilite vitamin, mineral and herbal supplement (the world's leading brand in that category), as well as Trim Advantage weight management and performance foods and XS Power Nutrition drinks. The "Personal Care" category includes Artistry cosmetic and skin care products (one of the world's top five brands in its category), Satinique hair care items, plus designer fragrances, bath and body lotions, soap and toothpaste — even jewelry.

In its "Store for More" feature, Quixtar lets you rethink your fashion wardrobe, revitalize your living space with bedding, furniture, and appliances, shop for lawn and garden supplies, vacuums, fitness equipment, and more. Leading brands include Liz Claiborne, Calvin Klein, Adidas, Fisher Price, and Sony.

You also can find great buys at Quixtar's "Partner Stores" — more than 100 of them. Better-known names include Barnes & Noble, Disney Store, Office Max, KBToys, Hickory Farms, IBM, Franklin Mint, Craftsman Tools, and Whirlpool. All of these products are available for doorstep delivery and, after affiliating with Quixtar, these companies saw extraordinary sales growth. This attests to the power of an e-commerce model based on affiliate IBO marketing, and to the efficiency of Quixtar's product fulfillment Biznet.

IBO Commission-Focused Value Pricing

Quixtar prices are competitively set to attract buyers as well as to generate a profit for the IBOs. Regardless of vendor or product, pricing strategy needs to be seen in proper context. This is particularly the case with an affiliate marketing company such as Quixtar.

Unfortunately, as brick-n-mortar retailing struggled to survive, consumers became brainwashed (by constant "sale" signs and "lowest price" claims) to seek out and expect to find what they perceive as bargains. But they bargain-hunt on the mistaken assumption they are saving money, when in reality they often are over-spending. They also tend to think — even though they've never closely checked into the matter — that some online product prices and/or delivery charges are high.

Big-box retailers, of course, are profit-driven. Their so-called discount or "lowest" prices are designed not to reward shoppers but to lure them, like dazed sheep, down aisles stacked with enticing but high-margin items, on which the store makes most of its profit. Shoppers in these stores are easily seduced into impulsive purchases — "into the bargain," so to speak — and end up with closets full of useless stuff. As I said, they over-spend.

Brick-n-mortar shoppers also totally overlook the hidden costs of shopping: gas for the car, wear and tear on the vehicle, and on footwear — and probably a coffee and snack. Such hidden expenses easily outweigh the delivery charge on an online shopping order.

Even then, true comparison shopping — based on total value, not simplistic blazing-red "buy-it-now" price stickers — should recognize *all* product facets: quality, utility, money-back guarantee, the convenience of home delivery, cost "per unit" or "per use," and so on. If you make fair allowance for demonstrable differences, you find that any product — if it is to succeed in the market over time — simply has to be competitive, no matter who sells it. And so it is with most Quixtar products.

To be sure, online shopping companies like Quixtar also are in business to make money. But, more to the point, so are their IBOs! These business owners think like business owners, not bargain-hunting shoppers. They want to offer high-quality products, competitively priced, on which they can earn a commission of up to 25 percent.

The beauty of the Quixtar model is that the IBO is not trying to convince new people to spend new money but rather to simply switch their existing spending (on products they genuinely need) to power their own Quixtar-powered business. They thereby earn an ongoing business profit for themselves, plus residual income for life and for their heirs, rather than constantly contributing to the shareholder dividends and pension funds of brick-n-mortar retailers.

IBOs thus prosper by changing their shopping habits — buying what they've bought all along, except now from their own Quixtar business rather than from elsewhere — and by getting others to do likewise. As a result, in its first four years online, Quixtar paid out $989 million in bonuses and incentives. A billion bucks and counting! As the old English shopkeeper's adage goes, "Keep thy shop and thy shop will keep thee."

Clearly, those successful IBOs believe prices are both competitive and fair. They know that they are the ones who really are getting the bargain, not the brick-n-mortar shoppers. And the products clearly are competitive because Quixtar, as mentioned, is by far and away the online leader in the entire health and beauty product category. Those sales speak for themselves, as do those in other product categories.

High-Touch Mentorship + High-Tech Tools

Like all good product-marketing businesses, Quixtar organizations have strong human resource skills development and training programs for IBOs, based on high-touch mentorship teaching and high-tech resource tools.

Mentorship is provided by those who've already built an extremely profitable business. It's an "experienced hands-on" process. The current business leaders in any affiliate marketing organization have a vested and ongoing interest in the business and financial success of every new IBO they register. This is totally unlike the so-called mentorship that might come from bosses in traditional businesses, most of whom only care about their own career success.

Successful IBO business leaders know what works and what doesn't, thus avoiding natural mistakes and saving new IBOs lots of time and trouble in building their business. The people who make the most money in affiliate marketing are those who spend lots of time developing those they register.

The Quixtar high-tech toolkit includes a variety of valuable books, CDs, and DVDs, plus high-touch product-education seminars and business-building conferences. These programs are the IBO's business-building support materials. IBO groups provide a tremendous decentralized Biznet platform for knowledge capture and sharing of expertise. In turn, this generates intellectual capital that develops professionalism among IBOs and leverages their business growth.

As such, the above blended "high-tech plus high-touch" program educates and motivates IBOs. It helps them grow professionally and personally, learning while they earn profits from their growing business.

One-to-One Community Relationships

Quixtar's high-tech website and business-building system also uses customer relationship management (CRM) software to track and understand shopper behavior, and to help maintain the trademark high-touch interaction provided by its network of super-enthusiastic IBOs.

Smart IBOs build their networks *offline,* channel their sales *online,* and manage their e-business both online *and* offline. Quixtar's success thus stems mainly from a breed of IBOs who understand how to build "high-tech plus high-touch" communities of customers.

They know that online success requires one-to-one, people-oriented, long-term customer-relationship building — plus cooperative teamwork and mentorship among IBOs. Quixtar's high-touch IBOs are the key differentiator that will lead it to success over most brick-n-mortar, pure online, and hybrid retail competitors.

Nobody outside of affiliate marketing incorporates this essential "human element" into their marketing strategies. Amazon, for example, can customize and personalize its website all it wants, but it still doesn't have human beings with whom you can interact and from whom you can learn how to succeed at growing a business. Wal-Mart, the planet's largest retailer, may have greeters to hand you a shopping cart, but that's as high-touch as it gets. Shopping in a sterile, cavernous, big-box warehouse like Costco or Sam's is neither high-tech nor high-touch. And how high-touch is your typical supermarket?

Pre-Existing Biznet Infrastructure

Quixtar launched with a significant leg up on its competition because it was able to plug in to an existing distribution, order-fulfillment, and customer service back-office platform or Biznet operated by Alticor, its parent company. That gave Quixtar access to eight highly automated, state-of-the-art distribution centers across the USA and Canada.

That strategic partnership also gave Quixtar a ready-made sales force of IBOs and an established product line — which they had already been buying offline, either in person from distributors or through a catalog selection that was as extensive as anything Sears Roebuck ever offered.

In launching its own products since, such as the XS sugarless energy drink that was first developed by a third-party "partner store," Quixtar also quickly slipstreamed new products into that Biznet distribution system.

The entire system is a behind-the-scenes Biznet with which the IBO interacts seamlessly through the Quixtar website and its Ditto delivery interface.

Word-of-Mouth Franchising, not Advertising

As mentioned, Quixtar does zero advertising. The model is based on the person-to-person and word-of-mouth business introduction and product endorsement of IBOs. All customer-acquisition costs are borne by the IBOs, who reap the rewards of business profits through the bigger gross margin that is available for disbursement through commissions and bonus incentives. From the IBO perspective, their operating costs are minimal and they access the Quixtar franchise and Biznet at zero cost.

The word "franchise" is very important here. In a legal sense, Quixtar does not operate as a brick-n-mortar franchise operation such as McDonald's. However, Quixtar IBOs are in fact akin to individual franchisees of the Quixtar model. They get a Quixtar franchise, with a full e-commerce platform, online shopping website, and Ditto delivery product fulfillment without any upfront cost. This is a proven turnkey operation that gives them a Webpreneurial start-up. And as they register more IBOs into their own business group, that is akin to building a chain of online franchise stores. They assemble and develop a network that is a sub-Biznet of the larger Quixtar Biznet.

Each IBO is loyal to the Quixtar website because, as explained, they earn a business profit from shopping there. This is the power of the affiliate marketing model of private franchising. Each IBO being loyal, they have no incentive to shop elsewhere. And being convinced users of the products, they confidently endorse them to others. Hence, each IBO business team, and the corporation at large, enjoys fierce customer loyalty and repeat purchase behavior that negates the need for advertising.

By the same token, as noted earlier with regard to product pricing strategy, neither is there need to resort to endless promotional campaigns and cut-throat price competition. On the contrary, Quixtar's premium-quality products basically sell themselves and earn each loyal IBO a fat commission check every month.

Undeveloped Marketing Potential

That said, I believe Quixtar IBOs could greatly benefit from a much more professional approach to Biznet brand positioning and product marketing. Here's why.

In the absence of advertising, few people other than IBOs have ever heard of Quixtar or its product brands. Quixtar is a private corporation made up of individual IBO businesses. By contrast, Avon is a public company that also does advertise, thus giving it a public profile. Quixtar grows through word of mouth and thus has no public profile, nor has it cultivated an online brand like Amazon or eBay. Hence it has no "brand equity" outside its loyal IBO base. Also, lacking even "halo" (corporate image) advertising, Quixtar drives traffic to its website only as a result of its IBO's efforts. IBOs would build the business more easily and faster with just a modest amount of corporate halo advertising to drive website traffic.

Indeed, while Quixtar got off to a very fast and impressive start, its sales are not keeping pace with total online retail growth. Yes, Quixtar is outpacing direct competitors, including Avon, which are slower and/or less competent in going online. And Quixtar is outpacing the market in health and beauty items. But the company is nowhere near fully capturing a broader and fairer share of many large and fast-growing online shopping opportunities that are now and will increasingly be available to it — and that its Biznet could readily handle.

The company's stated goal is to be among the "Top 5" global e-commerce retailers by 2010. I myself forecast in my year-2000 book *Future Consumer.com* that this would be the case. But Quixtar will only attain that level of performance once it markets more aggressively.

Getting into the top five also will require more IBOs to unequivocally embrace the e-commerce model, which many are too slow to fully adopt. For example, about 30 percent of Quixtar orders are still not placed online via the website but are phoned in to an 800 number. The recent website re-design will drive the percentage of online sales higher, as will the spread of computers and broadband access across society.

Still, only a relatively small percentage of orders are placed via the automatic "Ditto" replenishment process. Most IBOs still compose fresh online orders each time they shop. Not only is this cumbersome and inefficient from a product-fulfillment standpoint, it impairs efficient management, planning, targeting, and measurement of product sales performance — of the very PV on which IBO profit depends.

Consequently, the average IBO sales volume is nowhere near its potential. In fact, many IBOs are slow to switch their own personal shopping habits to a wider array of Quixtar products. Much of this stems from incomplete product knowledge and the lack of a coordinated marketing campaign to repeatedly focus IBO attention on product sales. As a result, other than when an exciting new product is launched, there is not enough focus on which products should be receiving more attention and stronger word-of-mouth promotion.

It is clear to me, as a result of hundreds of personal interactions with IBOs when I speak at Quixtar conferences, that they could easily triple their business volume overnight with a proper marketing focus — and I repeatedly tell them so. Moreover, they could grow their business two to three times as fast on an annual percentage basis.

More IBOs are gaining a better understanding of the market potential, some IBOs are growing much faster than average (thus showing what is possible), and the trends are moving in the right direction. So I do believe that Quixtar will get on a much faster growth path as e-commerce evolves and as more IBOs see the greater potential that is within their grasp.

Emerging Hybrid Business Development Process

Historically, affiliate marketing companies such as Quixtar developed their business through high-touch personal interaction. I believe that this characteristic is their unique strength and main point of differentiation. However, the Internet allows for a far more efficient, high-tech approach to business development, without sacrificing any of the high-touch. Some IBO teams in Quixtar are in fact now starting to build their organizations using the Internet itself. After all, this is a high-tech, Internet-based business that should be using more high-tech approaches to business development and human resource training.

IBOs now typically look for new business partners through pre-existing or referred personal relationships, among friends, family members, co-workers, and so on. However, this can be a haphazard approach that results in many people entering the business who really are not suited to it. As a result, they quickly realize their shortcomings, earn few commissions, and drop out. Yes, many new people will simply be clients or member shoppers at the Quixtar website. That is all well and good. But the majority want to be IBOs and build a home-based business backed by Quixtar's Biznet platform. And there is a major difference between being a passive online shopper and somebody who wants to grow a sustaining business organization. It requires entrepreneurial aptitude.

Some of Quixtar's more innovative IBO organizations are now using the Internet to search for and pre-qualify their new business prospects. Rather than talking to all and sundry about the business opportunity, these IBOs acquire vetted, "opt-in" e-mail lists of pre-qualified people who are seriously looking for exactly this type of business opportunity — people who want and expect to be contacted. The IBOs then screen these prospects and further pre-qualify them on a number of criteria to determine mutual interest, ability, and suitability. This process is conducted entirely online, before they finally meet with the best prospects face to face.

As a result of this hybrid high-tech/high-touch business development approach, these Quixtar organizations reduce their IBO turnover rate dramatically. This gives them far more time to focus on training and mentoring new IBOs and to focus much more on the other key dynamic of the business, product marketing and PV building. In turn, their average monthly sales volume per IBO is indeed tripling. And it is growing at double and triple the annual rate of some other Quixtar organizations that still look for new IBOs the old-fashioned way.

An additional advantage of online pre-qualification and IBO registration is that IBOs are not restricted by geography in attracting new IBOs onto their teams. Thanks to the "reversal effect" of the Internet, rather than the IBO having to seek out new business prospects, the prospects come to the IBO. All the particulars about the business opportunity are presented online via websites, webinars, and discussed or explained via e-mail and PowerPoint file exchanges, live Webcasts, and over the phone.

IBOs thus can build their globally networked, Webpreneurial Biznet from a distance. Their business is home-based yet global in scope, regardless of where they choose to live. Indeed, these Webpreneur families can easily relocate and still grow and maintain their Quixtar business unimpeded, with little or no need to travel long and time-consuming distances to do so. In turn, they will build stronger, more sustainable, easier-to-manage, faster-growing, and more profitable affiliate businesses.

Conclusions and Outlook for Quixtar

In affiliate marketing, Quixtar is far and away the leader — not only in most product categories but overall — and is running faster than its competitors. Its high-touch Biznet clearly is highly suited to e-commerce and is evolving as the leading hybrid of digital interaction combined with Webpreneurial relationships.

While it is difficult to forecast which websites will win out in some categories, those companies blessed with a first-mover advantage and Webpreneurial talent will dominate. As its IBOs become more Internet-proficient at business development and marketing, it now seems almost certain that Quixtar will at least be the top online affiliate marketer, and probably one of a small group of top online retailers in general. It is not yet a Webopoly, but it has the Biznet and human resource strength to become one.

Based on its success to date, other retailers need to take a close look at Quixtar's Webpreneurial IBO approach to marketing. I believe this form of private franchising is ideally suited to the Internet and will ultimately complement, if not replace, conventional forms of marketing and sales. As such, affiliate marketing would greatly enhance the marketing efforts of almost any type of business, including those of other companies examined in this book.

Strategy Lessons from Quixtar about Biznets and the "6 Ps" of Biznet Marketing

Biznet

- Launch your Biznet on a continent-wide "Big Bang" basis (that is, an overnight, full-system conversion), provided there is a critical mass of participants and a sophisticated distribution network already in place.

- Move fast, especially if you are a late-mover; there is still room for late-movers, if your model is unique and you adjust rapidly to the new market reality.

- Rapidly scale up a Biznet of solo Webpreneurs to create a global growth phenomenon with Webopoly potential.

- Use a sophisticated product-distribution and -fulfillment Biznet.

Mass-Customized Product

- Offer automatic order replenishment and delivery.

- Bring partner stores onto your Biznet platform to broaden out product offerings.

Any Place + Any Time

- Develop, manage, and market the business on a virtual, anytime/anyplace basis.

- Heavily decentralize an alliance or affiliate-based Biznet of solo Webpreneurs that is automatically self-organizing, economically elastic, and resilient.

- Use an affiliate marketing system of "private franchising" to grow your Biznet.

- Capitalize on the trend of people working from home.

- Offer a turnkey home-based business start-up opportunity.

- Offer websites in multiple languages to serve glocal markets.

Dynamic Value Price

- Charge value prices for good quality products that can be easily ordered and delivered.

- Make sure shoppers understand the hidden costs of brick-n-mortar shopping.

- Use value-pricing of products to support commission infrastructure.

- Use affiliate marketing as a "pay for performance" model, which is inherently well-suited to the Internet.

- Reward Webpreneurs with sliding-scale commissions, based on sales volume.

- Reduce customer and/or employee turnover by ensuring early and consistently growing income rewards.

- Do not waste money on unnecessary advertising.

Precise 1:1 Positioning

- Use word of modem and personal 1:1 connections to attract new business.

- Use "opt-in" e-mail prospects to build and market the business.

- Pre-qualify all customers, members, and Webpreneurs.

- Pre-qualify Webpreneur prospects, weeding out those who will only waste your time and are unsuitable to the business anyway.

- Use customer relationship management (CRM) technology to analyze shoppers.

- Focus on long-term customer relationships.

Personalized High-Touch Service

- Combine high-tech with high-touch in all that you do.

- Use high-touch marketing to complement the website in building the business.

- Invest heavily in human resource training and teaching/mentorship.

Profound Brand Experience

- Use personalized marketing and solo Webpreneurs, not mass marketing.

- Position the business as part of a Web Lifestyle that Webpreneurs understand.

- Tap into Webpreneurs' high personal investment in time/emotion to build loyalty.

Sears

multi-channel hybrid

We are going to leapfrog farther than
anybody else right now online. We're
starting where Lands' End is, and
pushing it farther.

—*Bill Bass*
VP & GM, Sears Customer Direct

SEARS IS THE WEB'S LEADING MULTI-CHANNEL MERCHANDISER.
The Webolution of shopping is the biggest change in retailing since
Sears, Roebuck and Co. launched its catalog in 1893. Having short-
sightedly shut down its catalogs in 1993, Sears floundered through a
department store slump until it found its way online — and thus,
importantly, back into its customers' homes! It has since revamped its
website and gradually broadened its online product offerings.

This new direction was mostly thanks to two factors. The first factor was the pioneering light shone on the multi-channel path to success by its subsidiary, Sears Canada, which retained its catalog and
thus its coast-to-coast network of local product pick-up centers. As a
result, Sears.ca has been Canada's number one retailing website since
2000.

The second factor was Sears' acquisition of Lands' End in 2002.
Lands' End was a leading catalog retailer that quickly and successfully made the online transition, with a website full of innovative features that made other retailers sit up and pay attention. This acquisition, along with the recent Sears merger with Kmart, should enable
Sears.com to jump ahead as a retailing powerhouse.

Sears.ca — First-Mover and Number 1 in Canada

Sears Canada (owned 55 percent by Sears Roebuck) is a multi-channel retailer, with a catalog, a website, and scores of full-line and specialty retail stores. Sears Canada has always been successful in the catalog segment, and it retained its books even after the company's main
competitor, Eaton's, closed its catalog operation. Perhaps not surprisingly, Eaton's later went bust.

Catalogs are part of Canadian culture, partly due to the extreme
winter climate that makes visits to stores sometimes difficult, especially for rural customers. When Eaton's closed down its catalog,
there was much bleating in the press about society's loss. Catalogs not
only make shopping easier, they also provide interesting fireside (and
bathroom) reading throughout the year, never mind winter.

More important, good catalogs can act as the "glue" that binds
customers to a particular store and engenders brand loyalty. In retaining its catalog operation — and by constantly refining it to make it
even more cost- and marketing-effective — Sears Canada retained a

local network of 2,200-plus customer pick-up centers that provided a perfect Biznet distribution infrastructure when it launched its Sears.ca website. Customers could select either to have the product delivered to their home, pick it up at a Sears store, or visit their local pick-up center (just as they had been doing all along with catalog or in-store orders). As needed, products also could easily be returned in the same way as before.

Sears Canada thus found it easy to persuade its catalog shoppers to move online and to gradually introduce online shopping to its in-store customers as they themselves went online and became comfortable with online shopping.

Today, Sears Canada's catalogs are distributed to some four million homes. Orders can be placed online, by phone, by fax, through stores, or at any of the 2,200-plus catalog outlets. More than 90 percent of these outlets operate under independent local ownership, as third-party agencies inside the likes of dry-cleaning stores or florists, with the remainder located inside Sears stores. Sears pays the agencies only a nominal fee; they gain the benefit of extra walk-in custom for their own business, drawn by the Sears sign on their storefronts.

This extensive Biznet places 93 percent of Canadians within a 10-minute drive of a Sears location. As a result, Sears charges next to nothing for home delivery. This ingenious network probably is the least expensive way to handle product fulfillment, maybe even as cheap as the "drop-off" stores that serve eBay customers.

Sears Canada also operates full-line department stores in most shopping centers across Canada. However, big malls are at market-saturation point in Canada and there are no plans to build more. Thus, other than building a few stand-alone stores, Sears Canada is pursuing growth through improvements to its catalog and online channels, and through its travel services division, which also operates online.

Sears Canada redesigned its catalog business in 2003, reducing the number of items offered, thus cutting inventory and avoiding stale merchandise. The company is further streamlining this operation to align it with the Sears.ca online strategy.

Easy-to-Use Website

First launched in 1996, Sears.ca was a content-rich website from the very start, giving it an appealing first-mover advantage. It applied its catalog-derived expertise of selling through pictures and text to quickly become the leading online shopping destination in Canada. Sales grew slowly at first, reaching $22 million in 1999 but jumping to around $100 million in 2000.

According to a year-2000 Retail Council of Canada study conducted by the big accounting firm Deloitte & Touche, Sears.ca was not only the number one Canadian website in terms of sales (ahead of Quixtar, Amazon, and eBay) but ranked number one for visits and customer satisfaction. Sears.ca also rated first in four product categories (toys, men's clothing, women's apparel, and appliances) and second in consumer electronics. Meanwhile, as we will see later, Sears.com in the United States was only selling appliances online.

By 2003, the site received 3.3 million visits, an increase of 22 percent over 2002, and grew just as strongly again in 2004. By the end of 2004, more than 84 percent of Canadian Internet users shopped online, representing more than half of the Canadian population. So the nation that grew up shopping on catalogs is now shopping digitally, often through Sears.

The Sears.ca site is well presented and easy to navigate, with colorful, detail-filled, and fast-loading pages, the latter especially with broadband access. The site was revamped and re-launched in 2003 with improved customer interfaces. Sears also made the website accessible through the Microsoft Network (MSN) shopping portal, thus allowing customers to compare Sears' products to those of other retailers.

Catalog-Rich and Store-Wide Product Range

By 2000, Sears.ca was offering the entire Sears Canada catalog assortment of 150,000 SKUs (stock keeping units) online, including tools and appliances of every make and description. At the time, it was North America's most comprehensive and authoritative product selection, with offerings far broader than even Amazon. And they were offered in both English and French, Canada's two official languages.

The site has nine major product sections on the home page, starting with fashion and accessories, baby needs, and "For the Home." These categories come first because women make or influence 80-plus percent of household purchases and they are the dominant Sears.ca shopping group. Indeed, more than 20 percent of Sears.ca customers are 25- to 49-year-old women who have household incomes over $60,000 per year. No wonder sales are booming.

Other website categories are appliances, electronics, "The Workshop" (tools), and fitness and leisure. The site also promotes Sears Canada's financial services category, with online applications for a Sears credit card and a co-branded MasterCard, plus the new Sears Canada Bank for which the company obtained a license in 2003. Links also are provided to Sears Home Central, Sears Travel, Sears Portrait Studio, and the flower shop, plus gift registry and "Wishlist" features.

Sears Canada Multi-Channel Infrastructure

By being the first major Canadian merchandiser to go online, Sears Canada was perfectly positioned, not only to capitalize on its brand name as Canada's number one merchandiser anyway, but to capitalize on the national online shopping trend as it gained momentum, as well as the trend of people working at home — thus making it easier to shop online and to accept deliveries.

To offer a seamless customer approach, the in-store, catalog, and online shopping operations are all integrated via a "back end" Biznet platform. Product offerings and delivery/fulfillment are identical to the user. As indicated, the online operation benefited greatly from the existing infrastructure of stores and catalog pick-up centers. So there was no change in product fulfillment, which is handled by a national network of 15 distribution centers and warehouses. Everything is coordinated over the Biznet, including communication with more than 2,000 different suppliers.

As a result, Sears Canada achieves a 98.5 percent accuracy rating on delivery times and further enhances customer satisfaction through its flexible product return options (in-store or at catalog pick-up centers). As well, online shoppers can check their accounts, track their orders, and receive confirmations. Order fulfillment is also confirmed through an automated voice message, alerting the customer that the product is available for pick-up. Delivery is free of charge to the pick-up centers.

Multi-Channel Shoppers Buy More

Sears Canada finds that customers are "cross-shopping" through the multi-channel options, depending on the type of product being bought.

The best example of this is in appliance purchases, where similar results have been achieved by Sears.com in the US. The site features almost 2,000 different appliance styles, with buying tips and product information, plus a feature that allows price comparisons. Most customers narrow down their choice of appliance and then bring related print-outs into the store to finalize their purchase.

In addition, customers who shop across channels typically buy more products. By way of example, let's say a person who only shops in stores spends $150, while a catalog shopper spends $100 and an online shopper spends $50. Then a cross-shopper who buys in stores *and* from the catalog, but *not* online, will spend $300. And a person who shops from the catalog *and* online, but not in stores, will spend $200. Moreover, a person who shops from *all three* channels will spend $400 or more. Indeed, the longer people have been shopping online, and the more new people there are who start shopping online, the greater the total amount purchased by each customer, both online and across channels.

In the late 1990s, Sears Canada's revamp of its catalog operation also enabled it to better segment its customers. Using customer relationship management (CRM) software, the company found that these high-value cross-channel customers represented about 30 percent of its catalog database. Hence, when Sears.ca went online, it was immediately successful and profitable. Online sales also helped to increase in-store sales, thus pulling the retail stores out of the industry slump that drove many department stores into bankruptcy.

In other words, far from cannibalizing in-store sales, Sears Canada found that the online channel re-invigorated those sales. By having retained its catalog, and having analyzed and computerized its catalog database, and then offering the same products online, Sears

Canada deepened its customer relationships and emerged as the dominant Canadian retailer, both overall and in all three channels.

Sears Roebuck and Sears.com

By contrast, when US department stores went into an economic funk, Sears Roebuck did not have its catalog business to fall back on. It also was late to go online and, when it did so, it only sold appliances. As a result, Sears Roebuck suffered a decade-long sales attrition while the big-box and specialty retailers — as well as superb catalog vendors such as Lands' End going online — ate away at Sears' customer base.

Indeed, other than its credit card database, Sears Roebuck basically had no clue about its customers. So, in ignorance, it tried slashing prices but naturally discovered it couldn't beat the discounters. As profits slumped, there was no money to modernize stores, nor to invest in vital e-commerce technology, and customer service also deteriorated. In contrast to its Canadian subsidiary, the entire parent company was stodgy, slow, non-innovative, and a downright unfashionable place to shop for almost anything.

In 2000, Sears.com added its Craftsman line of tools, then home, garden, and recreational equipment to the website offerings. These obviously were some of the toughest items to try to sell online because they are too bulky and expensive to ship. By mid-2001, Sears.com was getting only one-seventh the customer website traffic of Amazon, and no more business than Sears' own one-tenth-the-size Canadian subsidiary.

Nevertheless, Sears still was doing much better online than its main department store rivals, J.C. Penney, Kmart, Target, and Wal-Mart. By year-end 2001, some 30 to 35 percent of the products Sears sold online matched in-store offerings. The company began promoting cross-channel shopping with the slogan "Buy online; pick up at store." Sears was beginning to see that its online offering might be as successful as its now-discontinued catalog once was. But Sears.com still lacked a lot of spark.

Lands' End Re-Energizes Sears

In 2002, Sears Roebuck paid almost two billion dollars to acquire

Lands' End, a more upscale catalog vendor than Sears ever was, and a far more successful online retailer.

The Lands' End acquisition was a clear attempt by Sears to get back into the catalog business and to spruce up its dowdy online image. Lands' End already was the largest catalog and Internet specialty retailer. More important, it had a Biznet that was vastly superior to that of Sears.com.

Last, but certainly not least, Sears acquired the expertise of Bill Bass, who headed up Land's End's online efforts. Sears placed him in charge of the company's entire e-commerce effort, now called Sears Direct division. His mandate was to give Sears.com a complete make-over, integrate it with Lands' End, and converge it with in-store offerings — just as Sears Canada had done — to create a seamless, multi-channel customer experience.

The old Sears.com site was so slow and so poorly organized that it was decided not to list any Sears merchandise in Lands' End catalogs or on its website. To begin, only a few Lands' End products were placed in Sears stores. Other than cross-links between the two websites, there was no product or shopping integration. Everything had to operate separately until Sears.com could be revamped.

This process took almost a year before Bass rolled out the new site in late 2003. After a major redesign, graphic and information content was increased by a factor of five, but the new pages downloaded up to seven times faster than the old site. The site was far better organized, with products laid out more cleanly, and was far easier to navigate. Thanks to new caching technology and the use of a lighter HTML code, Bass commented, "we saw a dramatic improvement in speed and customer satisfaction the day the new site went live."

The new site and the online product database was now fully integrated with the inventory in Sears' nearly 700 stores so that customers could order online and pick up at a local store later the same day. By 2003, monthly website traffic grew to 20 million visits and overall sales for Sears.com reached $300 million. While this was still far behind the biggest Internet retailers, Sears was clearly now getting it right.

Still, there was a huge void in Sears.com offerings. Apparel, for which Sears was once noted and for which Lands' End was well known, had to wait until 2004. But when the new website's next phase came, it had all the bells and whistles.

"Virtual Model" and "Virtual Room"

Lands' End is famous for pioneering the use of virtual reality technology on its website with what it calls a "virtual model," where customers can insert their measurements, and even their own photo, to virtually "try on" clothing. To take advantage of that technology, in 2004 Sears added apparel to its website and the feature allowed customers to "try on" multiple brands of clothing.

Sears then extended this feature to other categories, creating a "virtual room" where shoppers can see how paint, paintings, wall hangings, tables, lamps, window treatments, floor coverings, and bed comforters can be arranged to redecorate their bedroom. Other rooms such as a "virtual kitchen" were then and still are progressively added to the site. Thus home furnishings and kitchen appliances and dishware also became new product additions in 2004.

Both these "virtual" features allow the customer to zoom in and focus on fabrics and textures. Online shoppers also can switch colors for all product illustrations, not just on the virtual model.

Rapidly Expanding US Product Range

As a result of these innovations, about 50 percent of Sears' apparel offerings and some 70 percent of its home furnishings products are available on Sears.com, and more are being added constantly. The initial focus was on best-selling items, and 2004 sales were up about 40 percent over the 2003 level, growing even faster than the 28 percent increase for online shopping at large. Today, Sears.com offers far more products than any single Sears store could possibly keep in stock.

Sears' move into apparel was well timed to take advantage of increasingly strong growth in online clothing sales. Pioneered by Lands' End before it joined Sears, the apparel category is now second only to computers and electronics in terms of overall online dollar sales volumes. And apparel is a category that e-commerce critics said would never succeed online because the customer needed to "see, touch, feel, and try on" the merchandise.

As is turning out to be the case in every online product category, the skeptics are again being proven wrong. Industry forecasts are for online sales of apparel and accessories to reach at least $12 billion by 2008 in the United States. And Sears.com intends to get its due share.

Sears' move into online apparel sales in 2004 follows a move by Wal-Mart in 2003 to again try to sell clothing online, something it abandoned in 2000. Amazon also launched an online apparel category in 2002. But Lands' End proved beyond a doubt that there was a large and growing market for clothing, particularly as the available technology kept advancing so that a website could be more user-friendly for this more tactile product.

A major economic advantage of selling clothing online is that the product return rate is much lower than for store-bought clothing. Only 10 percent of apparel bought online is returned by the customer as unsuitable. This is slightly more than double the return rate for online merchandise in general, but much less than the 25 percent return rate for store-bought clothing. And, of course, the items can easily be returned to the store.

Another Easy-to-Use Website

The revamped Sears.com website is organized somewhat differently than that of Sears.ca, with Amazon-like tabs across the top of the page for major product categories. These tabs are for appliances, baby, clothing, computers and electronics, for the home, jewelry, lawn and garden, sporting goods, and tools. There are also a search feature and links to the clearance center and auctions.

Immediately below that, the site blares out "Free Shipping" and then prominently promotes three or four items that are on sale. This is a good merchandising feature in that those items constantly change, so the site always has a fresh appearance to returning customers. But these promotions take up more space than the ones on the Canadian site.

As a result, Sears.com lists all its departments down the left-hand column in a menu format with sub-categories. That makes the site look somewhat cluttered compared to the Canadian site. But who am I to argue with Bill Bass. It's probably just that my wife and I are familiar with the Sears.ca site, which we duly admit using frequently.

One valid criticism of the Sears.com site, though, is that the link to Lands' End is in tiny print at the bottom of the page. In my opinion, that brand should be prominently displayed, and Sears and Lands' End should be aggressively cross-selling each other's merchandise.

On the plus side, Sears does use the website to test-market various products. For example, a digital music player piloted online was so successful that it was quickly rolled out in stores. In this and other ways, Sears clearly is leveraging the cross-channel marketing power of the Web to complement what its refurbished stores do well, thus further refining its evolving multi-channel Biznet strategy.

Biznet Distribution System

By better harnessing the power of the Web, Sears changed and solidified relationships with both its suppliers and its customers. The company is driving down costs, improving levels of customer experience and service, and collaborating better and more efficiently with its business partners.

Paper-based processes are being digitized to occur in real time. The company has used its Biznet to take the industry-standard process of collaborative planning, forecasting, and replenishment (CPFR) to another level. CPFR forces real-time information sharing among importers, manufacturers, and transportation companies. They come together in a Biznet that allows real-time tracking of products, order fulfillment, and shopper activity.

Online shoppers, of course, make shopping decisions at any time of day or night about what to buy and their preferred delivery and pick-up times. In turn, by using customer relationship management (CRM) software, Sears can study customer buying habits and product purchases, allowing it to calculate lifetime customer value and develop personalized product promotions. In effect, order fulfillment and customer satisfaction become more effective, but at much lower cost.

Co-incident with the acquisition of Lands' End in 2002, Sears was in the process of modernizing its information technology (IT) infrastructure with help from Dell and other IT partners. Sears installed streaming media technology for videoconferencing and to smooth and speed up other operational tasks. It also began using this IT infrastructure for online employee recruiting and in-house training.

In its huge 24-hour-a-day distribution centers — some are more than one million square feet in area — Sears also upgraded the logistics of its warehouse order-picking system. It introduced handheld devices to conduct price checks and manage inventory, all via its Biznet. Using a wireless network with one central database server in each warehouse, it also fitted out all its forklifts with color-coded touch-screen terminals. The forklift driver's order-pick list appears on the screen and instructions are updated as each item is picked.

Software and product changes can be made instantly, on a Biznet-wide or warehouse-by-warehouse basis. The drivers adapted to the new Biznet easily because, as one company executive observed, "they already use the Net at home; this is a cinch for them."

And that speaks volumes, not only about the ease of use and proficiency of Sears' Biznet but about the future growth potential of online and multi-channel retailing.

Conclusions and Outlook for Sears

During 2004, Sears reported that more of its customer base was shopping online and that its sales were growing by 40 to 50 percent over the prior year.

While Sears clearly is not yet a Webopoly, thanks to the Lands' End acquisition and the merger with the refinanced Kmart, it is well positioned to be a dominant multi-channel retailer. If Sears can arrange additional similar strategic investments, it will considerably broaden its market potential and growth rate.

To become a Webopoly, Sears Roebuck needs to learn more from Sears Canada and develop strategies that get many more of its Sears and Kmart customers online — and to do so quickly before Wal-Mart gets its online act fully together.

The future of mass merchandising in North America likely will come down to a three-way mass-merchandising battle among number one online retailer Amazon, number one multi-channel retailer Sears, and number one brick-n-mortar retailer Wal-Mart. The biggest spoils will go to the company that creates the highest level of customer satisfaction through a seamless Biznet. But a more determined Sears could grab that mantle, at least in North America.

Strategy Lessons from Sears about Biznets and the "6 Ps" of Biznet Marketing

Biznet

- Be a late-mover online, provided you rapidly adjust your Biznet to the new market.

- Integrate all channels through one common Biznet database for customers and products.

- Integrate collaborative planning, forecasting, and replenishment (CPFR) into the Biznet.

- Digitize every employee position, from CEO to fork-lift driver.

- "Clone" and extend your Biznet channels to other branches of the company.

Mass-Customized Product

- Offer limitless product selection and variety of choice.

- Offer the same products across all channels.

- Do not be afraid to cannibalize sales; online excellence will boost overall sales.

- Encourage "cross-channel" shopping to boost sales.

- Use lots of multimedia content to present product offerings.

- Optimize your search engine to allow customers to quickly find what they want.

- Use the website to test-market new or modified products.

- Realize that the "touch and feel" of the product is not a barrier to online shopping.

Any Place + Any Time

- Pursue a click-and-mortar, multi-channel strategy: stores, catalog, and online.

- Maintain catalogs as another touch-point/point of entry directly in the customer's home.
- Start a catalog, or acquire an established catalog retailer.
- Transition catalog and/or in-store shoppers online as quickly as possible.
- Allow customer pick-up/drop-off at physical channels.
- Establish a coast-to-coast network of customer pick-up/drop-off centers.
- Provide all customer interfaces and product information in languages other than English as required by market conditions and customer expectations.

Dynamic Value Price

- Use the Biznet to constantly drive down costs and boost efficiency in all channels.
- Offer free delivery to pick-up centers.

Precise 1:1 Positioning

- Use customer relationship management (CRM) software to study customer buying habits and product purchases to then develop personalized product promotions.
- Use virtual reality to allow customers to "try out" products such as clothes and furniture.

Personalized High-Touch Service

- Capitalize on the social trend of people working from home, thus making it easier to shop online and accept doorstep deliveries.
- Use the Internet for recruiting and in-house training.
- Ensure the website maintains the brand's standards, but is fully adapted to the differing needs and expectations of online shoppers.

Profound Brand Experience

- Harmonize channels to offer a seamless customer experience across all channels.

- Offer personal notification of all online orders when they are ready for pick-up.

Tesco
"glocal" grocer

From time immemorial, people have wanted their groceries delivered. We didn't have to heavily sell the service. We now have a proven business model. And we don't go into a market unless we can be the leader.

—*John Browett*
CEO, Tesco.com

TESCO IS BY FAR THE WORLD'S BIGGEST ONLINE SUPERMARKET. Where others failed to take groceries online, Tesco is quickly, successfully, and profitably rolling out an online grocery ordering and direct-to-home delivery model in one country after another. It now blankets its native United Kingdom and Ireland, and is moving rapidly to grab the leading online supermarket position in Europe, North America, and Asia.

Tesco.com thus represents the "second coming" for online groceries. And this time it is working. Tesco developed a Biznet that taps the pent-up consumer demand for online grocery shopping and home delivery. This consumer demand is so universal that if Tesco continues to get it right it will gain global Webopoly status very quickly.

First Get it Right, Then Roll It Out Fast

Tesco did not have the first-mover edge in online grocery shopping. In fact, Tesco.com's CEO John Browett is somewhat dismissive of the idea, arguing that speed to market in and of itself is insufficient. He says, "First-mover advantage has two parts to it: being first and getting it right. There are loads of examples where people forget the second bit."

The first online grocery shopping services were in the United States, but most of these dot-coms became dot-bombs or failed to execute fast enough or effectively enough. The most notable failure was Webvan, which, as I wrote in my book *Future Consumer.com*, probably had the distribution model that will most likely succeed in the long run. Webvan, I wrote, "has proven that there is a demand for online grocery shopping and, given time, I am sure that either Webvan or somebody else will make it work as a profitable and successful business."

Webvan clearly was not too early; there was a huge pent-up demand for its service in many markets — particularly in the high-tech areas of the US west coast where it first launched — and its delighted customers were dismayed when the company suddenly folded in 2001. But Webvan's plans were far too ambitious. A pure dot-com start-up, it blew through $1.2 billion in capital, both on trying to build out a national distribution center Biznet, and on advertising. It simply ran out of money before it could build a big enough national customer base.

Some of this was due to the fact that customers are slow to change their shopping habits. So in that sense, Webvan was too early to try to do what it was attempting on a national basis.

By contrast, companies such as Chicago-based Peapod (now owned by the Dutch supermarket conglomerate Royal Ahold) provided a service whereby Peapod took online grocery orders and picked the products from local-partner supermarkets. Peapod is still around, but it has not grown to anywhere near the size of Tesco in the UK because it does not have its own dedicated network of supermarkets.

Tesco.com essentially followed the same Peapod model in Britain, except that it picked products from its own national network of supermarkets. This store-based model meant Tesco could expand online fast and with low overhead. Tesco determined early, as Webvan learned too late, that it would need to deliver to a very large customer base and not simply a wide geographic area to justify a dedicated set of warehouses for the online business channel. Only now is it starting to build a distinctly separate online product distribution system.

Actually, Tesco started developing its online grocery model much earlier than Webvan, in 1996. So it certainly was a first-mover in that respect. However, determined to "get it right," Tesco took its time. Six middle managers were put on the project and told to work it out from first principles: using existing Tesco strengths (brand, supermarket network, marketing ability, and company ethos) and insisting on short-term profitability while focusing on how to be the big, long-term winner in the online channel.

The model was first tested at a single store in West London and was gradually tweaked until it worked as well as possible. Once a workable prototype was developed, says Browett, "we rolled it out very, very fast." This progressive roll-out and build-up of the Tesco.com Biznet began at the end of 1999. It now utterly dominates the UK online grocery shopping segment. In fact, Tesco already is the largest online grocer in the world.

By contrast, Tesco's main UK supermarket rival, Sainsbury's, tried to set up a separate, Webvan-like warehouse model for online grocery shopping. Sainsbury's lost millions of pounds on warehouses. This again shows that execution (getting it right and then moving fast) is far more important than big and grandiose plans, whether or not you already have an existing supermarket business.

Conversely, Tesco's carefully measured zeal to be number one was successful. Its tried and tested e-commerce model quickly became hugely popular and was profitable by 2001. Tesco.com's sales of almost £600 million (about US$1.1 billion) in 2003 were still only a small percentage of total company sales. But the business is growing at a rapid clip, is attracting customers away from competitors (both online and into Tesco stores), and is allowing Tesco to extend its brand across a wider range of products and services.

Extensive Product Range

Tesco's website is looking more like that of Amazon a couple of years ago, with category tabs spreading across the top of the page. As with Amazon and its books, the first tab on Tesco's site, of course, is groceries, followed by finance and insurance, telecoms, wine, electronics, DVDs, videos, CDs and games, flowers, and then — guess what? — books.

And there lies an interesting parallel in how the two companies extended their brands across an ever-increasing array of product categories. Amazon first developed a book business and then diversified into a host of categories including, at one time, groceries. Tesco started with groceries and did the same, and it argues that groceries are much better at building customer relationships than any other product — again, "if you do it right" — because, quite simply, everyone needs to eat. Since food is bought frequently, it quickly fosters loyalty to a superior-value supplier such as Tesco.

Even before going online, Tesco was Britain's dominant supermarket chain and its number one gasoline retailer. It also is a major Internet service provider in Britain. Hence it had a huge, very loyal, and tech-savvy existing customer base to draw upon. From the start, it thus aimed to leverage that base, plus the frequency with which people shop, to build an online business where half the sales come from higher-margin non-food products rather than lower-margin groceries.

Tesco is a fearless entrant (offline and online) into new product categories, many under its own private-label brand names. They include consumer electronic products (such as TVs, PCs, DVD players, cameras, and cell phones); home appliances, furnishing and lighting products; crockery, cutlery and cookware; vases and glassware; towels and linens; toys and sporting goods; discount clothing; health and beauty products; flowers and gifts; books and music downloads; wine and champagne; telecom and Internet access services, travel services, and a host of financial and legal services. You can even buy your household gas and electricity through Tesco and, in 2004, it launched its own in-store satellite TV channel called TescoTV (discussed later).

With this awesome product range, it is not surprising that by the end of 2004 Tesco's share of the total UK non-food market had risen rapidly to almost 10 percent versus its industry-leading 31 percent share of the entire grocery sector. Some categories are growing as fast as 40 percent per year. And in the online channel, it was second only to Amazon (UK) in non-food items.

Price Leadership: "Pile It High; Sell It Cheap"

Tesco has always been a price leader. The company was founded by Jack Cohen, who began with a grocery stall in London's East End in 1924. He went on to open his first store in 1929, on the eve of the Great Depression. To survive, Cohen always bought in bulk and kept costs and prices low. His motto was, "Pile it high; sell it cheap," and this later became the title of his autobiography.

Ever since, the company has been driven by high quality, low prices, convenience, and a satisfying customer experience. It even accepts discount coupons issued by its main rivals. In 1993 it introduced its own line of lower-priced private-label goods. And in 1995, as discussed below, it launched a heavy but very successful personalized coupon program that adds to the customer value proposition.

Tesco still managed to carefully move up-market, taking business away from higher-priced competitors, by adding higher-value and luxury products to attract a different clientele. In turn, that stood it in good stead with online shoppers because they tend to be premium buyers. But Tesco still remains the value proposition leader.

Tesco remained the value leader when it went online. Unlike the warehouse delivery models, by having products picked from nearby stores, Tesco customers get their usual products at the same localized prices. While ordering online, customers also can do instant price checks and are alerted to current price cuts, which Tesco can implement or change at a moment's notice. As well, orders over £99 get free delivery, thus encouraging people to order more. This makes the entire process more cost-efficient and allows Tesco to reap economies of scale.

Strategic Product Partnerships

Tesco launched some of its higher-value products and services in conjunction with strategic partners. In financial services, for example, it launched a co-branded Tesco Visa card. But its main Tesco Personal Finance portfolio of products was launched in a 50–50 joint venture with one of the UK's most innovative companies, the Royal Bank of Scotland. This service now has about five million account holders and offers some 20 different products — from savings accounts to mortgages to traveler's checks — either in the physical store, by telephone, or online via Tesco.com.

Every store has at least one banking machine and, at in-store checkouts, customers can access their bank accounts online. They also can buy instantly effective insurance for their pets, their holiday travel, their automobiles — even breakdown coverage for their car should it stall as it leaves the parking lot. Tesco also sells life insurance, and more than 30 percent of Tesco's overall insurance sales occur online.

In 2003, in partnership with cell-phone service provider O2 and its own Home Phone service, the company launched Tesco Mobile. The handsets are sold online or in the stores, and nearly one million subscribers have already signed up. They get cheaper service, from a trusted company, and also earn points on Tesco's Clubcard loyalty program every time they make a phone call.

One-to-One, High-Touch Market Segmentation

Tesco's online shopping experience is closely tied in with the company's Clubcard loyalty program, started in 1995. By 1996, 200 million purchases per day were tracked by the Clubcard program, and more than 5,000 customer "needs" segments were identified. Each segment began receiving personalized coupons based on this customer relationship management (CRM) system. Tesco's coupon redemption rate is an astonishing ninety percent versus an overall retail industry average of three percent.

Using CRM, Tesco analyzes each customer's buying habits and draws their attention to goods or offers that are most likely to interest them. This personalized cross-selling effort has been a major factor in its success, both in boosting customer satisfaction and in growing company profits.

Tesco also found that the top one hundred customers in any store were worth about the same as the bottom four thousand in terms of profitability and lifetime value. Moreover, the top five percent of customers account for twenty percent of sales, whereas the bottom twenty-five percent of customers represents only two percent of sales.

This further helps the company segment its market. Different lifestyle magazines are published for different segments of customers. High-value customers receive personal phone calls from the store manager to show appreciation for their business. They also get valet parking when they come to shop, and other special privileges. Similarly, expectant mothers are given priority parking and personal shopping assistants to help them; parents with newborns have change room facilities.

These high-touch efforts at delighting the customer have further boosted Tesco's brand image, market share, and profit. When the company offered online shopping, many of these delighted high-value customers were naturally the first to log on for the service.

Supermarket TV

TescoTV was launched in 2004 in partnership with Hughes (a unit of DirecTV) and some of its partners. This project does not relate directly to Tesco's online shopping venture, but it is instructive about the company's innovative approach and how it perceives the Biznet future. Indeed, there is no reason why a concept similar to TescoTV could not be applied to the company's website and be streamed to individual website pages or to individual online customers on their TVs, PCs, handheld devices, or cell phones.

In essence, Tesco views retailing as a multi-channel multimedia content business. The Digital Retail Network division of Tesco is headed up by a Media & Revenue Generation Manager. Name one other supermarket — or any kind of retailer — that has such an executive!

As an in-store network, TescoTV displays news and entertainment, as well as promotional information on both Tesco private label and other brand products. Third-party product suppliers pay Tesco to promote their products on TescoTV and these advertising revenues more than cover the cost of content creation and system operation.

Tesco finds that 70 percent of in-store buying decisions are made at the point of sale. The company believes customers benefit from timely educational material about products, particularly if they are waiting in line at the checkout. They also get to enjoy non-promotional content such as cooking instructions, cartoons, and other entertaining content, as well as a revolving news channel much like CNN.

The system delivers varied program content to different areas of Tesco's stores, displayed on about 50 flat screens of various sizes. In the Café area, customers watch the latest news, sports clips, and entertainment content. The latest music videos are shown in the Home & Entertainment and Health & Beauty departments.

Thanks to sophisticated multimedia authoring, editing, and scripting tools, any content can be changed at will and then re-sent to all stores or any in-store department within minutes. Schedules can be changed in real time to send customized content across the store on an individual screen-by-screen basis.

TescoTV doesn't just pay for itself, it boosts sales by at least 10 percent, almost regardless of product category or brand. The system also is a great help in bringing new products to market quickly. Esthetically, shoppers say it enhances their shopping experience by increasing their product knowledge, alerting them to new products or product improvements, all while keeping them entertained.

Imagine, as I suggested, how powerful this would be in the online world. While you shop online, you could be entertained with the latest music, videos, cooking clips, or any other product-related content

— similar to how Amazon now shows short movies on its website to help sell products. Then shoppers might choose to add that new DVD or new cookie recipe to their virtual shopping carts, all for prompt delivery to their homes.

Profitable Home Delivery Process

As mentioned at the outset, when Tesco went online in 1996 it relied on its network of existing stores to pick-and-pack-and-deliver groceries to the home. It did not build new warehouses or distribution centers. As a result, the total start-up costs for Tesco.com were a modest £30 million (about $58 million) spread over four years. Later it spent a few million more to expand the online offering to include non-food items.

Shoppers can order by phone, fax, or over the Internet — the latter now accounting for most orders. Before the Internet became widespread, Tesco experimented with grocery catalogs (first printed ones, then on CD-ROM) so that customers could compile their shopping list offline. Today, the shopping website is programmed to remember the shopping list to make repeat ordering easier and much quicker once the initial list is compiled. The Tecso process for this is almost identical to Quixtar's "Ditto" system.

Unlike Quixtar, however, which uses automated distribution centers, Tesco's order-fulfillment process is very similar to simply doing the customer's grocery shopping for them in person. When an online order comes in to Tesco, it is automatically forwarded to the supermarket nearest to where the customer lives and is kept on a computer server at that store.

As mentioned, the range of products and prices available to that online customer is managed by special software so that the products and prices match exactly what is found in the store where that customer would otherwise physically shop. In other words, Tesco is a glocal grocer and, as such, each store in effect has its own online storefront.

Orders are filled by staff working in shifts, each team of pickers filling the orders for a series of two-hour delivery time slots. Pickers push a computer- and scanner-equipped "wireless" trolley around the store, gathering up items on the order lists of up to six customers.

The trolley is guided through the store by its onboard computer so as to bypass high-traffic areas at certain times of the day whenever possible, thus avoiding jamming up areas filled with offline shoppers. To further speed the process, Tesco divides its stores into six picking zones: groceries, produce, bakery, chilled, frozen, and "secure" (items such as cigarettes and wine).

The trolleys have six sliding trays, each identified with a sticker showing one customer's order number. As items are picked they are scanned and placed in the appropriate customer's tray. Simultaneously, the Biznet updates in-store inventory and triggers new product shipments from the warehouse and, in turn, from suppliers.

On average, each item takes 30 seconds to pick and scan, so that a 60-item order is filled in 30 minutes. On average, however, only 10 items per customer come out of each zone, so that six partial orders are filled from each zone every 30 minutes.

As the six partial orders for each zone are completed, they are taken behind the store and consolidated, on a customer-by-customer basis, directly into waiting delivery vans. The vans make 12 deliveries per run, three runs per day, organized around two-hour time windows selected by shoppers.

Profitable within a Short Period

Is Tesco making money at this? You bet. For starters, the cost of order picking, including labor and depreciation on equipment, is covered by the delivery charges. Tesco also saves on labor costs by requiring fewer checkout clerks to serve in-store customers.

As well, online order lists tend to be about three times larger in value than in-store shopping lists. This is because customers want to get as many items as possible delivered at one time. They also feel the need to order sufficient to justify the delivery charge that, as noted, is free if they order more than £99 worth.

Furthermore, products bought online tend to have higher gross profit margins (due both to the type of product selected as well as their more efficient fulfillment), thus boosting Tesco's net profit on the online service even further. On top of that, a full 50 percent of Tesco.com's customers previously were not Tesco patrons, so their orders represented significant new sales volume. And by eventually selling a wider range of products, Tesco did not cannibalize in-store sales.

Thus, with an enhanced Biznet, a few in-store pickers, and a gradually expanding fleet of delivery vans and drivers, Tesco rolled out its online grocery shopping and delivery service, one store after another — and did so profitably. After the one prototype store near company HQ in London, the project was extended to a pilot program involving first six, then eleven stores. Finally it was rolled out rapidly to one hundred stores in 1999, and then faster still until it blanketed the entire country — all while using its existing distribution center network.

Tesco.com showed its first profit in 2001 and has never looked back. As company CEO John Browett said at the time, "For us to scale up the business is easy. If we double our orders, we buy more trucks." In 2002, he said Tesco could do at least 10 times as much online business before causing a logistical problem in stores or needing to build separate warehouses. However, he did estimate that, before reaching such a capacity, Tesco would evolve towards using warehouses in dense urban markets, while still continuing to use the store-picking model for rural customers.

State-of-the-Art Distribution Center

Tesco moved in this direction, partnering with Tibbett & Britten to design, build, and operate for Tesco the busiest and most sophisticated distribution center in Britain. Located at Thurrock in Essex, not far from London, its 495,000 square feet of space has about two miles (3.2 kilometers) of aisles full of 45,000 stacked pallets. It can handle 2.5 million cases of food products a week and it has 64 loading docks where a truck arrives and departs each minute on a $24 \times 7 \times 365$ basis.

The distribution center is almost entirely paperless and a central part of Tesco's Biznet. It has 7,500 picking slots and uses radio frequency identification (RFID) technology for scanning goods coming in, being picked, assembled, and shipped out. Pallets and cartons are identified with RFID tags, which are much like bar codes but which emit radio signals of the product code. Picking directions are issued from traffic stations in the loading bays, from where data are downloaded to RFID terminals worn on the pickers' arms. In 2005, Tesco will rollout RFID readers to all its UK distribution centers and stores to track pallets and cases of goods.

To optimize product flow, items are differentiated by characteristics such as rate of sale and cubic volume. Products are also picked at the warehouse into color-coded totes that match the zoning used in the in-store pick-and-pack operation. This speeds up and avoids any excessive movement of faster-selling items, both in the stores and in the distribution center. It also hastens the cross-docking of the trucks, where products come in on one truck and go back out again on others.

Each truck is integrated via GPS satellite–Biznet links to manage both the order capture and delivery route planning processes. Full route and job details are downloaded to the driver's handheld terminal in the vehicle's cab. This helps ensure maximum fleet availability and usage. This one distribution center alone eliminated two weeks' inventory from Tesco's supply chain and increased on-shelf product availability.

As Tesco's new Biznet evolves, its 30 regional distribution centers will be modernized or replaced in this way. The entire set-up is managed by regional directors, one per center, via a sophisticated network of PCs connected to the Biznet. And every Tesco supplier is linked into the Biznet so that they can see exactly which of their products is selling, both online and in-store, on a real-time basis.

The Tesco online shopping system is now so sophisticated that, as discussed later, the Safeway chain has adopted it in North America. Tesco itself is rolling it out in other countries where it operates, notably in Ireland and South Korea, with great success. As other companies struggle to succeed online, it is highly likely that Tesco, like Amazon and eBay, will start to license out its e-commerce platform and/or form strategic partnerships to implement it with other retailers. In fact, CEO John Browett has publicly indicated as much.

High-Touch Employee and Customer Service Focus

While obviously a high-tech company, Tesco focuses lots of energy on human capital and invests heavily in training and motivating its employees to raise the customer's shopping experience. For example, it uses its TescoTV platform to deliver learning modules to employees, or simply to communicate with them about company or product changes.

One of Tesco's main training programs, called "Living Service," is designed to encourage all employees to live the corporate value slogan, "No one tries harder for customers." More than a thousand Tesco managers have gone through a related leadership development program. And in late 2004 the company's in-house training program was accredited by the UK Qualifications and Curriculum Authority, which means that Tesco can award the five-level National Vocational Qualification (NVQ) in retailing to its staff.

These human asset investments are paying off on the bottom line, making Tesco a hugely profitable company by UK and North American supermarket standards. In turn, it offers employees the chance to join its profit-share and "Share Save" schemes after two years of service, with shares allocated based on the number of hours worked. Employees can save up to £250 per month, and those who joined in 1998, for example, had earned a £49,000 value by 2003 — tripling their money.

Tesco's stated core purpose is "to create value for our customers; to earn their lifetime loyalty." And two sets of values drive the way it does business: "No one tries harder for customers"; and "Treat people how we like to be treated." To these ends, managers are taught to properly look after their employees so they, in turn, can properly look after the customer. Employees are constantly encouraged to understand customers better than they understand themselves, and to be energetic and first for the customer.

Extremely Satisfied Customers

To satisfy customers, Tesco pickers select produce as if they are shopping for themselves. When online grocery sales first began, of course, the skeptics said people would not use the service, particularly for fresh produce. They said people wanted to "squeeze the tomatoes" to be sure they got good quality and the exact ripeness of produce they preferred. That turns out not to be the case, as Webvan proved before it flamed out, and as Tesco has proven again.

In fact, at least 90 percent of the people who say they need to touch and feel the produce don't have a clue what they are doing when they do the sqeezing. And, as Tesco also found right from the start of its service, the most popular items ordered online are, in fact, fresh fruit and vegetables. Go figure!

If a Tesco customer wants a mixture of green and yellow bananas, or all green or all yellow, she can so specify. The pickers simply have to do a good job to maintain customer satisfaction, and so avoid complaints and returns.

Indeed, Tesco's online shoppers get *better* produce than if they had selected it themselves. Tesco goes to extreme lengths in picking and packing its home deliveries. Egg cartons, for example, are bubble-wrapped for extra protection. Such touches only serve to assure customers they are getting good quality products and service. Not only are customers impressed, they tell friends and neighbors about it, resulting in more business for the online store.

Some industry skeptics also doubted there was sufficient customer base, outside of maybe affluent high-tech areas, to support the growth of an online grocery business. They feared that most customers were too set in their ways to change their shopping habits. Again, while shoppers can be slow to change, if a change is a logically appealing no-brainer, people will eagerly switch to a new way of doing things. Thanks to its excellent model, Tesco.com proves these skeptics to be dead wrong. It is drawing customers from every segment of society and every geographic region.

Particularly noteworthy is the appeal of online grocery shopping to retirees. In the rural Yorkshire market town of Skipton, for example, numerous senior citizens went out and bought a computer just so that they could shop online when the local Tesco went online!

The store manager said that 80 percent of those who bought a computer after Tesco.com's launch in Skipton were beyond retirement age. In other words, online grocery sales helped drive computer sales. Normally, it would be the other way around. Tell that to the skeptics!

This episode illustrates just how good Tesco's service is, and shows the level of customer satisfaction Tesco.com enjoys. The world's supermarkets had better wake up.

Out-of-Touch Supermarkets

As a result of Tesco's proven success, the stodgy North American grocery industry is now being forced to take another look at online shopping. After all, supermarkets sell replenishment, commodity items, ideally suited to online retailing. And supermarket profit margins in North America are a meager one to two percent, with weekly sales of only $11 per square foot — which barely covers the cost of the real estate.

Unless supermarkets go online, as I told grocery conferences years ago (always to a largely in-denial audience), somebody else will get it right and will put them out of business — just as Tesco is doing to its rivals in Britain.

Most supermarkets are digitally challenged. They were late to adopt bar-code scanning, never mind selling online. And, as Webvan and other online grocery start-ups spotted, the entire supermarket distribution system is way behind the times and extremely vulnerable to being made obsolete by a modern-day Biznet.

Yet, in a recent survey, only 14 percent of US supermarkets thought home delivery was important and only 20 percent were in the least bit worried about online competition. Well, they'd better start changing, because Tesco has landed in America.

Safeway and Tesco in USA-Canada Online Partnership

Safeway and Albertson's are the only North American supermarket chains to make any realistic attempt at online shopping. But in 2001, Safeway joined forces with Tesco to bring workable online grocery shopping to the continent, using the winning Tesco model described above.

Safeway has struggled endlessly with online delivery, seemingly unable to get it right, trying one thing after another. It first tried Internet sales in 1993 in conjunction with Peapod, but that program was cancelled due to high costs. In 1999, Safeway started testing its own online system in California. It also tested office delivery without much success. Safeway also tried self-scan checkouts for customers, then ordering by phone or fax for customer pick-up, then it gave customers handheld computers to send in their order lists. None of these models worked. And the constant changing only served to confuse employees and customers alike.

Then Safeway acquired GroceryWorks.com, a dot-com start-up that operated in Texas, as its online channel. GroceryWorks also had been going in fits and starts, having built two special distribution centers (like Webvan) in Texas for home delivery that failed and were suspended.

So impressed was Safeway with how well Tesco had succeeded, it asked Tesco to be a strategic partner in GroceryWorks. Tesco took a 35 percent stake in the business for $22 million. Now operating as Safeway.com, it is rolling out the Tesco model along the US west coast, picking products from local Safeway and/or Vons (owned by Safeway) supermarkets.

The project began in Portland (Oregon) and then Vancouver (Washington), later spreading to Seattle, then down to Sacramento and the San Francisco Bay Area — Webvan's old stomping ground, where customers were delighted to have online grocery delivery available again. Later it added Southern California and then Las Vegas to its market coverage. By mid-2004, Safeway's online sales had doubled since the Tesco-system roll-out began in mid-2002, and the company said it expected online sales to double again in 2005.

The combination of Tesco's intellectual and Biznet know-how about online groceries with Safeway's brand is perfect for bringing online grocery shopping to the world's largest market.

By the end of 2004, Safeway was running neck-and-neck and head-to-head with Albertson's in building out its system across the western USA. Albertson's uses a similar online model, picking and delivering groceries from its own local stores. It claims to serve a larger market area than Safeway, extending its service into Pennsylvania in late 2004. But my bet is that Safeway will run faster and better, and will cover the continent first.

As to the rest of the competition, the only other major player is Royal Ahold's Peapod. But that operation has slowed down because of a variety of corporate management and financial troubles within the Dutch-controlled parent company, and Peapod is losing money anyway. Publix closed its poorly run online operation and itself has gone into bankruptcy protection. Most surprisingly, neither Kroger nor, more astonishingly, Wal-Mart offer any online grocery ordering and delivery. Like I said earlier, they still don't get it.

Conclusions and Outlook for Tesco

Even without these laggards, online groceries are back in North America and growing strongly, with sales expected to top seven billion dollars by 2008. That will still only be about one percent of total grocery sales, but the online segment is growing by about 50 percent a year and slowly but surely eating up market share. The first online grocery wave failed, but it proved the customer value proposition. It took Tesco to prove that the online business worked. It now is no longer a matter of whether Internet grocery can be successful, but rather how big it will become.

Webvan tried to reinvent the grossly inefficient grocery industry in one fell swoop; to do so, it had to create a huge logistics company, but failed. Tesco used its own existing and super-efficient infrastructure to keep costs low, using the Internet as a new channel to serve existing patrons and attract new ones from slow and inefficient competitors. It created a click-and-mortar hybrid to first build a profitable business base.

Tesco's main UK competitor, Sainsbury's, was slower to begin online operations and went the dedicated distribution center route. It simply dropped farther behind and lost still more market share to Tesco. The number three UK supermarket chain ASDA, owned by Wal-Mart, only delivers to selected areas, again from dedicated warehouses. Both these Webvan-like models are proving ineffectual against Tesco, both due to inferior management, higher fixed costs, smaller revenues, and a logistical nightmare.

By the end of 2004, Tesco.com was processing a record 600,000 online orders a month. Tesco is achieving what dot-com upstart Webvan and established supermarkets failed to do. And, determined to be the leader in every market it enters, it seems destined to be not only the world's leading online grocery retailer, but perhaps one of the largest online retailers of any type of product — maybe even books. It's another Webopoly Biznet in the making.

Strategy Lessons from Tesco about Biznets and the "6 Ps" of Biznet Marketing

Biznet

- Aim to be first in every market you enter.

- Move fast, especially when you are a late-mover; there is still room for late-movers who get it right.

- Get it right, then roll it out fast. Develop a prototype and test it to get it right. Do a small-scale pilot project, then scale up fast.

- Insist on early profitability by thinking through every process of the Biznet model, while focusing on long-term market domination.

- Use existing distribution network infrastructure until volume grows.

- Target and leverage the tech-savvy segment of the existing customer base first.

- Quickly build a critical mass of loyal customers.

- Use radio frequency identification (RFID) technology for scanning/picking products.

- Warehouse the products based on rate of sale and cubic volume.

- Use color-coded skids and tote boxes for the same product items across the system.

- "Clone" and extend your Biznet to other products and markets.

- License out the Biznet platform to other companies.

Mass-Customized Product

- Extend the brand online and across a wide array of product lines.

- Initially use printed catalogs and CD-ROM catalogs to list product offerings.

- Offer an easy-to-repeat ordering system on the website, so that customers can readily update and submit their orders next time.

- Form strategic partnerships with selected leading brands to offer complementary services.

- Use digital media content to bring new products to market quickly.

Any Place + Any Time

- Offer limitless product selection and variety of choice.

- Realize that the "touch and feel" of the product is not a barrier to online shopping.

- Use well-selected perishable products, which benefit from fast delivery, to enhance the consumer appeal of the service.

- Realize that online shopping does not have to cannibalize in-store sales but rather can boost them.

- Capitalize on the trend of people working from home, thus making it easier to shop online and accept doorstep deliveries.

- Capitalize on the booming segment of retirees who appreciate online shopping and welcome home delivery.

- Make doorstep delivery a profitable proposition; ensure there is enough local population density and/or a nearby source of product, to make home delivery economic.

- Localize your online product range to match that of local stores.

- Warehouse and distribute products regionally, managed by regional directors.

- Have idling trucks waiting to deliver customer orders in batches, based on delivery-time windows.

- Use GPS satellite links via the Biznet on trucks to simplify delivery logistics.

- Base the Biznet on individual stores to make it resilient and scalable: more nodes can be added rapidly without strain, and at minimal incremental cost.

- Give each brick-n-mortar outlet its own online storefront.

- Perceive the business as being a multi-channel multimedia content business.

- Use content to target product messages at consumers, in-store and online.

- Launch in-house streaming-media satellite TV capability to carry informative and entertaining content to customers; partner with sponsors to cover the cost.

Dynamic Value Price

- Be the price leader: "pile high, sell low."

- Provide comparisons with competitors' prices on your own website.

- Accept discount coupons of competitors.

- Change prices in real time.

- Localize online prices to match those of local store offerings.

- Perfect your logistics, thus allowing you to afford price reductions.

- Offer free delivery on orders over a minimum value.

- Appoint a "Media & Revenue Generation Manager."

Precise 1:1 Positioning

- Use customer relationship management (CRM) software to segment customer base.

- Use personalized cross-selling techniques.

- Publish different lifestyle magazines aimed at selected customer segments.

Personalized High-Touch Service

- Incorporate human values in your business and marketing strategies.
- Use in-house TV for employee communication and training.
- Have a profit-sharing scheme for all employees.
- Offer valet parking to high-value customers.
- Make personal phone calls to high-value customers.

Profound Brand Experience

- Go to extreme lengths in picking and packing to ensure customer satisfaction.
- Cultivate long-term customer relationships.
- Use a customer loyalty program.
- Ensure that "no one tries harder for customers."

Outcome
biznet strategies

Every business will be an e-business . . .
or it will not be in business.

— *Andy Grove*
Chairman Emeritus, Intel

THE ECONOMY IS BEING RECONFIGURED BY THE WEBOLUTION into a digital economy. Implicitly, business must be digitally competitive to survive and prosper. The Biznets examined in this book clearly show that the digital economy is starting to coalesce around a limited number of market leaders, or Webopolies. Biznet Webopolies will have a far greater impact on commerce than did the Industrial Revolution.

The Internet significantly changes how to most effectively build, operate, and market a business. Some companies "get it," but many don't. There are too many mediocre managers in charge of too many dinosaur businesses who are either ignorant of the threats and opportunities of Internet technology or are leery of even the slightest change. Yet they must Webify or die.

Biznets become winners because they organically plug into Webolutionary market forces. They operate with exceptional efficiency and customer-focused responsiveness, thus differentiating themselves with irresistible value propositions and superior product offerings. Our six Biznets show that wealth is not to be gained by endlessly trying to fine-tune old ways of doing things but by seizing and perfecting a breakthrough strategy that changes the rules of the game.

The overall strategic advantage of a tightly integrated and superbly managed Biznet is that it is a self-reinforcing system that perpetuates its own growth and raises huge barriers to entry against competitors. Any competitor wishing to be a "fast follower" by imitating a Biznet strategy must not only replicate the whole system but also operate it at least as effectively as the original first-mover. The digital world simply demands a new strategy as to how a business is structured and managed, and how it interacts with strategic partners and customers — a Biznet strategy.

Biznet Strategy Drives Corporate Strategy

The greatest threat to an established company lies not only in failing to leverage the Internet but in failing to deploy it as a strategic Biznet. Biznets are real-time business networks that use the Internet not only to become super-efficient but to deliver exceptional products directly to online customers and so amass a dominant market position. Only those companies that muster the kind of strategic leadership shown by the six Biznets in this book will prosper in any meaningful way.

The lesson from Amazon, eBay, Dell, and Quixtar is that e-business perhaps works best in its pure, customer-direct, online-Biznet form. Hybrid click-and-mortar retailers are not as successful because they tend to hesitantly straddle both channels; they saddle themselves with two sets of overheads and struggle with channel conflicts. However, Tesco overcame that double-edged challenge by building its online presence out of its stores, and by linking the two channels through a seamless Biznet. Sears did the same by first leveraging its catalog clientele online, then linking all three channels through a seamless Biznet.

These six Biznets send a clear signal to pure brick-n-mortar retailers. Biznets meld systems and relationships over an interactive platform that allows for personalization, customization, instant ordering, and overnight delivery. No brick-n-mortar retailer will ever compete with such awesome power. Big-box operators such as Wal-Mart, Costco, and Circuit City are at the zenith of brick-n-mortar retail. Unless they move online, seamlessly through a Biznet, they will find themselves trapped inside a walled-up cul-de-sac — dead-enders whose time is up.

Online retailing is the breakthrough channel of 21st-century retailing. As more and more customers shop online, it will be their preferred channel for easy-to-buy and easy-to-ship products. And we likely will see a few Webopoly vendors constantly take business away from change-resistant traditional retailers.

Simply investing more in information technology (IT) and opening up an e-commerce channel are not enough. In his book *Business @ the Speed of Thought*, Bill Gates estimated that even those companies that do invest heavily in IT are realizing only 20 percent of its potential benefits. The only serious digital competitor will be an e-business with a Biznet strategy that underpins and subsumes overall corporate strategy, not vice versa. The CEO must be the Chief e-Business Officer, whose task is to Webify and digitize the company.

In other words, corporate strategy must have a simple focus: to be the number one Biznet in the industry, aiming for Webopoly status.

Biznets must network the entire organization and link it in real time with suppliers and customers. It must be a virtual organization that operates in real time and focuses on real-time information and streaming multimedia content, not products. The objective is to gain an overwhelmingly dominant Webopoly position, pre-empting new entrants and thwarting competition.

The table on pages 132–33 summarize the strategies of the six Biznets. The remainder of this chapter discusses these summary findings in slightly greater depth.

Biznet Design and Operation

The table readily shows that these six successful Biznets have several design and operational features in common, as follows:

• e-Business (not e-Commerce)

To begin, it is abundantly clear from even a scant review of these six Biznets that an e-business is not the same as e-commerce. A Biznet is an enterprise- and industry-wide extension of e-commerce. More than that, it breaks the existing industry and business mold.

• First and Fast in Building Critical Mass

A winning Biznet strategy is to be first, fast, flexible, cost-effective, super-efficient, and vastly superior at rapidly building a critical mass of customers, which serves as a huge barrier to entry. In turn, as eBay, Amazon, and Dell show, such Biznets develop strong customer loyalty, superior value, and high profit margins.

• Super-Efficient and Productive

As Dell abundantly demonstrates, Biznets offer huge operational and competitive advantages: lower costs, product customization, faster time-to-market, zero components inventory, awesome/flawless assembly, super-efficient market reach, 1:1 targeted promotion, immediate transaction completion, and prompt product delivery.

• Partner-Driven

All six Biznets use strategic partnerships of one sort or another. Biznet-linked suppliers share and leverage their core competencies in making superior-value products available directly to consumers on a one-to-one product "pull" basis. Today, creating strategic Biznet relationships is almost as easy as clicking on a partner's website icon to cross-link the websites. Biznets also bridge the gap between suppliers and customers by sharing real-time information about customers' purchasing habits and changing needs. Biznets allow everyone to work from a common customer relationship management (CRM) database to ensure 100 percent satisfied customers.

• Glocal and Webpreneurial

Winning Biznets attune their operations, their websites, their products, and their service offerings to local and individual markets on a global basis. While all six of our Biznets are glocal, eBay and Quixtar epitomize the Webpreneurial future of commerce. eBay facilitates worldwide person-to-person commerce. Quixtar effectively uses affiliate marketing as its Biznet strategy, and it is not alone in this regard. Some of the biggest corporations use this model to great effect. Just two examples are MCI and Sprint, which grabbed retail market share from AT&T by signing people up through "friends and family." While MCI and Sprint experienced some financial problems, their network marketing model finally won the battle, in that AT&T completely abandoned the residential phone market in 2004.

• Harmonized Channel Transition

Tesco and Sears show us that traditional retailers can successfully make the transition to online selling, provided they smoothly integrate all their existing channels, leverage them as their initial Biznet platform, and rapidly move their existing customer base online. Quixtar even went online with a "Big Bang," overnight transforming its products and Webpreneurial IBOs to a brand-new product purchasing and fulfillment mode. So there is no excuse for all those old-time retailers who are too afraid to take the plunge into the future that is inexorably appearing before their eyes.

Winners Use the "6 Ps" of Biznet Marketing

The six Biznets also succeed because of their marketing strategy. At the beginning of this book, I outlined the "6 Ps" of the Biznet marketing

Biznet Features and "6 Ps" of Marketing Strategy

	AMAZON	eBay	DELL
BIZNET FEATURES	Visionary; big goal; 1st-mover, scale fast; e-Biz competencies; customer critical mass; real-time, fast response; product partners; glocal Biznet; clone/lease out Biznet.	Virtual company; network of Webpreneurs; rapid scale-up; user critical mass; real-time transactions; product partners; glocal Biznet; license Biznet to others.	Break industrial mold; 1st-Mover, selling direct; lightning-fast assembly; customer critical mass; real-time, fast response; strategic component partners; clone/extend Biznet.
MASS-CUSTOMIZED PRODUCT or SERVICE	Millions of products; content about products; customer product "pull"; customer self-orders; precise search engine; "1-Click" ordering.	Content infomediary; handle no products; category management/ marketing; optimized search engine; person-to-person trades.	Each customer "builds to order" online; customer in control; 1st to market with latest-feature products; cross-sell related items.
ANY PLACE + ANY TIME	Glocalized websites; reach buyers at home; open 24 x 7 x 365; many delivery options; super logistics/delivery.	Glocalized websites; reach users at home; open 24 x 7 x 365; virtual agora/bazaar; seller handles fulfillment.	Glocalized websites; Reach buyers at home or business; open 24 x 7 x 365; super logistics/delivery.
DYNAMIC VALUE PRICE	Price leader; bundled offers; free delivery over a minimal amount; collect revenue before paying suppliers.	Dual-pricing (auction bidding or fixed); free membership; modest fees for listings; broker products to obtain high gross margin.	Low-cost assembler; value-price/quality leader; free upgrades/shipping on all orders; zero inventory; negative cash conversion.
PRECISE 1:1 POSITIONING	Suggest other products based on personal purchase history; engender referrals.	Serve solo Webpreneurs; part of user Web Lifestyle; engender referrals via feedback/ratings.	CRM to track behavior, aid service/segmenting; personal websites for "Premier" customers.
PERSONALIZED "High-Touch" SERVICE	Personal "welcome" page; rapid e-mail service response to queries; personal "Wish List"	Leverage "social capital" of user community; obsess about user feedback; teach users how to sell.	Solve user problems; digitize solutions and "fix" them online; outsource onsite service.
PROFOUND BRAND EXPERIENCE	Put customers at center of their own universe; be on "Favorites" lists; be ranked #1 overall in "customer respect"; become a "love" brand.	See through users' eyes; empower users, adapt to better serve them; tap emotional investment of user community; be on "Favorites" lists.	Measure satisfaction; forums for "Premium" customers; bulletin board for buyer feedback and to answer queries.

QUIXTAR	SEARS	TESCO	
"Big Bang" launch, if there is existing critical mass of customers/ distribution system; move fast, especially if late-mover; rapidly scale up network of solo Webpreneurs.	Late-mover, but adjust very rapidly; quickly transition catalog shoppers online; learn from subsidiaries; integrate channels via CPFR process; digitize every position.	Be #1 in any new market; first, get it right; then roll it out very fast; insist on early profitability; use existing distribution until volume grows; Web-savvy shoppers first; build critical mass.	BIZNET FEATURES
Wide range of products; partners broaden range; let customer self-order; precise search engine; automatic repeat order replenishment.	Wide x-channel range; let customer self-order; virtual "try on" ("see-feel-try" is non issue); optimize search engine; use Web to test market.	Wide array of products; use catalogs/CD-ROMs until website ready; localize product offerings; easy-to-repeat online ordering.	MASS-CUSTOMIZED PRODUCT or SERVICE
Glocalize websites; home-based franchise of Webpreneur affiliates; open 24 x 7 x 365; super logistics/delivery.	Multi-channel operation (store, catalog, Web); retain or start a catalog; open 24 x 7 x 365; local pick-up centers.	Pick-pack-deliver orders from nearest store; give each store its own online storefront; 2-hour delivery "windows."	ANY PLACE + ANY TIME
Value-priced, high-quality items support affiliate pay-for-performance commission structure; low fee for members; do not advertise.	Competitive pricing; drive down costs; special online discounts drive website traffic; free delivery to local pick-up centers.	Price leader; same prices online/at local store; show competitor price comparisons online; free delivery over minimum order value.	DYNAMIC VALUE PRICE
Personal connections and word of modem; opt-in online recruiting; high-touch, 1:1 marketing.	CRM study buying habits, develop 1:1 promos; "Virtual Model" helps personalize products.	CRM to segment market; 1:1 cross-selling; lifestyle magazines for different segments.	PRECISE 1:1 POSITIONING
High-touch mentorship/training to develop IBOs; hybrid high-tech/touch sales and service.	Capitalize on "work at home" trend; use Net for recruiting/ in-house training.	Human values ethos; employee profit sharing; valet parking/phone calls to high-value clients.	PERSONALIZED "High-Touch" SERVICE
Tap Webpreneur's time/ emotional investment; position business as part of Web Lifestyle; pride of owning profitable family run e-business.	Seamless channel integration from customer perspective; personal notification when online orders ready for pick-up.	Go to extreme lengths to pick-and-pack produce to ensure 100 percent buyer satisfaction; "Club Card" program; "No one tries harder."	PROFOUND BRAND EXPERIENCE

mix and suggested we would find that the leading Biznets were successful, not just because of their technology platform, but because they used each of these "6 Ps" in their marketing strategy. As summarized in the above table, that clearly turns out to be the case. So let's run through the "6 Ps" in a bit more detail.

Mass-Customized Product

Manufacturing is shifting from mass production to mass customization. Already, tens of millions of customers configure their own products online. Inevitably, hundreds of millions of consumers will eventually do so, and point-and-click prefabrication of everyday items will become the rule rather than the exception. To survive, factories, warehouses, and distribution centers must be melded into an integrated Biznet facility that operates at the beck and call of online shoppers.

Biznets also make the market for specialized products much larger than before. As Dell shows, mass-market products can now be mass-customized for markets of one. Conversely, even low-volume items can find a mass market. For example, 57 percent of Amazon's sales come from 2.2 million non-best-selling books that individually sell so few copies, brick-n-mortar stores don't even carry them. And almost all of eBay's person-to-person sales are of one-of-a-kind items.

As well, Biznets present and market products through the medium of content. The higher the product content, the easier it is to configure and evaluate the product online, and to precisely attune it to individual consumer tastes.

Any Place + Any Time

In the future, the brick-n-mortar store will be less a place for selling products and more a showroom — with smaller inventories of broader product offerings — that will also serve as a product pick-up and return center. Whatever channel model they choose, retailers must realize that a meaningful online presence is much more than printing a website name on their shopping bags. To compete, they need a Biznet like those of Sears or Tesco.

Biznets are open on a 24 × 7 × 365 basis globally, thus reaching potentially billions of customers with localized offerings. They use superlative logistics and product fulfillment operations to speedily take products right to the customer, at minimal cost.

Dynamic Value Price

Biznets are dynamically fluid marketplaces that lower the cost of both innovation and marketing. In the digital economy, the previously high price of economic scarcity is overwhelmed by the constantly shrinking costs of plenty, largely driven by the phenomenon of ever-better and constantly cheaper microchips. Chips flip the cost-price equation, not just for PCs or consumer electronics but for any manufactured product. In parallel, the Internet makes it possible to invent and develop better products faster than they are commoditized, and to market and deliver them at lower cost. As such, the economics of a Biznet are compelling.

The relatively low overhead of e-tailing is a huge cost advantage over brick-n-mortar stores. To reach a market of 10 million potential customers it costs a traditional retailer about one billion dollars in capital investment. Conversely, an online retailer can reach the same market for only one million dollars — 99 percent less capital investment. It thus took Wal-Mart 12 years and 78 stores to reach $150 million in sales. Amazon did it in three years, with one website, one warehouse, and an initially narrow product range. And while Barnes & Noble and Borders combined have more than 2,100 stores, their 21 percent (and dropping) share of the book market compares with Amazon's 19 percent (and rising).

Operating costs also are much lower online. For example, it costs a high-volume retailer about $2.50 to process a catalog order versus pennies for an online order. Overall, conventional marketing is now five times more expensive than e-marketing. Again, Biznets clearly win and, regardless of channel strategy, most retailers will be forced to rationalize their brick-n-mortar presence, ultimately closing as many as 80 percent of their outlets to survive.

Biznets that rapidly ramp up thus find themselves with more and more buyers who spend more but who cost incrementally less to service. Such Biznets harness the Web to track data on what customers buy and then cross-sell and up-sell additional products to them. Biznets also gain pricing power over manufacturers, by sharing customer data with them. Also, since online price comparison is easy, this forces prices down and, in turn, gives more leverage to the low-price leader.

Biznets also offer dynamic localized pricing, with bundled offers, free upgrades, free shipping, and modest service charges — whatever it takes to maximize the customer value proposition.

Precise 1:1 Positioning

Consumers have never before enjoyed so much power. Online customers exercise a huge amount of leverage and choice over vendors. Biznets meet this challenge by allowing the company to establish 1:1 relationships and boost the customer value experience. Each customer is "one in six billion." Customers are as different as their fingerprints and behave as individually as their genes. And the Web is a perfect medium to both customize and personalize offerings, thus fostering lifelong relationships.

Biznets allow the customer to exercise control through round-the-clock self-service options. In turn, this reduces operating costs and errors. Customers also expect to continually gain better value and service from their vendors. Biznets allow companies to meet this expectation through an irresistible offering of better-quality and latest-edition products that are personalized to each customer's needs. And through personalized access to the Biznet, customers can readily determine delivery status and be fully informed throughout the fulfillment process.

Satisfied customers tell others about their brand experience, one by one. Just as word of mouth was the most effective mode of product promotion in pre-Industrial times, so is word of modem the most effective mode in the Internet Age. Word of modem replicates exponentially, squaring its online reach in accordance with Metcalfe's Law of networks.

Hence, mass advertising broadcast to everyone is a complete waste. It merely hypes products with millions of dollars that not only inflate prices but do not guarantee even a single sale. Word of modem is sent as a personal recommendation to only those people whom the sender believes, based on knowing them, will be interested in the product.

The use of customer relationship management (CRM) software ensures one-to-one, personally relevant marketing messages and product suggestions. Biznets literally get to "know" their customers through CRM. They build profiles about each customer's interests and then target specific, opt-in product information to them. CRM considerably boosts customer loyalty and retention. The cost of retaining a customer is essentially zero, whereas the cost of finding a new customer is expensive. CRM builds long-term, personalized relationships and lets the company focus on life-time value, not one-time sales. After all, each and every CRM file is a profit center.

Personalized High-Touch Service

Customer-centered companies leverage "relationship capital" through extraordinary customer service and consistently satisfying shopping experiences. Biznets leverage the "social capital" of communities to which customers belong.

Personalization adapts content to each customer's expectation based on their CRM profile. Research shows that a website with customization and personalization can grow its customer base by as much as 50 percent a year and its revenues by about 55 percent. Moreover, customers who use these features are five times more loyal.

Examples of these features are Amazon's personalized "Welcome" greeting and product "Suggestions," Quixtar's "Ditto" automatic re-order process, and Dell's "Customize It" automatic product-configuration process.

Biznets also obsess over feedback from customers and strive to communicate with them immediately about any and every query. They use high-touch approaches with both staff and customers in order to build strong and enduring loyalty.

Profound Brand Experience

For service-obsessed customers, the shopping experience is at least equally as important and as valuable as the product they buy. Only with a Biznet can a company manage the customer brand experience effectively.

The first online customers were techie geeks who were quite at ease with even the clunkiest of websites. Today's mainstream customers are much different; the website must be easy to use, convenient, efficient, and give shoppers a highly satisfying and memorable experience — like driving an open-top convertible on a sunny day with a light breeze down a not-too-busy main street, hitting green lights all the way. If they enjoy the "flow" of the ride, 80 percent of them will "bookmark" the site onto their "Favorites" list and will come back repeatedly for another trip.

Online consumers demand instant satisfaction or they quickly move to another website. In such a click-intensive environment, is it possible to build and maintain a brand online?

Brands are built in the consumer's mind. A great brand monopolizes "share of mind." It is seen as the category leader, customers feel comfortable with it, and it delivers what the customer expects. The Internet is the most powerful medium for communicating the essence of a brand in an in-depth, personalized way, creating an experience that grows richer with time. As repeat website visits occur, a bond of trust is created that fosters consumer intimacy with the brand.

In the old world of "mass" (mass production, mass consumption, mass advertising), companies and their brands became impersonal. In an attempt to stand out in a crowded marketplace, brands presented a single, monumental message to a mass market. But consumers, bombarded by ads for look-alike products, didn't get that message, and those brands lost ground. Web brands, by contrast, offer context to a global multitude of individuals. The key difference between old and new branding, then, is the need to connect with consumers through one-to-one relationships and with personalized context rather than through a mass-marketing blitz.

As Amazon says, branding thus must put the customer at the center of his or her shopping universe. The intimacy of the Internet allows brands to become relevant to each customer through personalized experiences, rich content, and customized products. This allows companies to capture the consumer's imagination at lower cost and to generate repeat business. Biznets build such intimacy by putting control of product and service information directly into the customer's hands via the website.

All six of the product-diversified brands studied in this book use the Internet to create a special value proposition of high credibility and repute. They became brand leaders, showing that the Internet is a great leveler that can rapidly lift new brands up alongside long-established brands, and even put them in a leadership position.

Amazon, eBay, and Dell, for example, are Biznets that created their brands from scratch — directly with individual customers, one customer at a time, entirely online. They also started with a single product. Amazon initially focused on books, dominated that category, and then extended the brand across numerous categories in rapid succession. eBay focused on one type of business (auctions) in a few products and then rapidly broadened that out. Dell started with PCs and is broadening its brand to cover more types of consumer electronics.

The other three Biznets discussed here — Quixtar, Sears, and Tesco — were existing general merchandisers that had thousands of products to begin with. They show that an offline brand is a valuable asset in creating an online brand by seamlessly weaving products and channels together so that the loyal customer can interact either online or offline.

All six Biznets empower their customers, users, or Webpreneur affiliates. They tap into and leverage the emotional commitment of each of these community groups to the brand. These Biznets simply go to extreme lengths, in everything they do, to please their clientele. And they would not be able to do that if they were not Biznets.

Conclusion

Biznets are the future of business. They are the way of the world. And they break the mold. In the future, every company either will be its own Biznet or part of somebody else's — otherwise it will wither and die.

The starting premise of this book was that Biznets are amassing Webopoly power that threatens to lock out slow-moving or lesser-integrated e-business market competitors. Some of the six Biznets are already at or approaching Biznet Webopoly status. They meet the four Webolution-driven criteria described at the outset:

1. Fast growth at low and declining marginal cost.

2. Exponential growth from less investment capital.

3. High value generation through the fast and far movement of content.

4. Extended market reach, from the individual to the global.

Our six Biznets are relentlessly driving down costs towards zero and exponentially expanding their market share towards infinity. They are exemplars of "zero-infinity" Biznet Webopolies in the making. And the rest of the global business community faces hard choices and tough questions if it is to try to emulate them before it is too late. I hope this book will both spur them to action and help facilitate their strategic direction.

To that end, the book concludes with an Appendix of strategic e-business questions to brainstorm and consider. I urge every business to not only become an e-business but to grasp the promise of its Biznet future. It's right there waiting for you, in your imagination.

Strategic e-Business Questions to Brainstorm and Consider

A. Biznet Strategy

1. What is our e-business vision and mission?

2. How do we become an e-business?

3. How can we become a virtual and a glocal organization?

4. How might we best Webify our organization?

5. What will it take to become the Webopoly of our sector?

6. Are we going to be a first-mover or a fast follower?

7. What are the things we must *not* change or abandon?

8. What aspects of our conventional wisdom do we need to question and/or get rid of?

9. What are we best at? What are we worst at? What new capabilities do we need?

10. How do we become a "zero-infinity" company?

11. Do our IT systems have enough speed, robustness, and scalability?

12. Do we have staff with the appropriate awareness and expertise of new and future technologies?

13. Where will our competitors come from?

14. How well are we differentiated from our competitors? How does the Internet change points of differentiation?

15. How might we become more digitally competitive?

16. How do Web economics change our business model?

17. What is our "value web" and how can we enhance its value to our customers and ourselves?

18. How might we take advantage of "winner take all" economics?

19. If "everything gets reversed" by the Webolution, what does that imply for us?

20. Who are our strategic Biznet partners going to be?

21. Which intermediaries can we eliminate? What new mediation roles might we play?

22. Are we going to be a pure clicks retailer or a click-and-mortar hybrid? What role, if any, will bricks play in our e-business?

23. How can we tap into the Webpreneurial phenomenon?

B. Products and Production:

1. Who will be the winners in our product category?

2. If all products are merely content to be experienced, what are the implications for our products in a context-centric world?

3. Which of our products are most suitable for online sale, why, and how might we make them more suitable for that?

4. How do we ensure we are always first to market with the latest products?

5. Can we be the price leader?

6. Which, if any, of our products are vulnerable to online can-

nibalization, and what should we do about that?

7. Which of our products are in danger of being commoditized?

8. Are any of our products destined to become museum curiosities?

9. What brand-new, previously impossible product offerings does the Internet open up for us?

10. Can our products be mass-customized online and, if so, how?

11. What products or processes are we able to digitize, either partially or completely?

12. Is our supply chain well enough integrated, internally and externally?

13. Are our supply partners plugged in well enough to our customers?

14. How can we drastically reduce if not eliminate inventory?

15. How can we drive costs towards zero?

16. How well do we provide product fulfillment?

C. Customers and Marketing:

1. What are our "6 Ps" of marketing?

2. How can we achieve exponential revenue growth?

3. How do we best achieve critical mass?

4. What are the implications for us if 70 percent of families are living a Web Lifestyle by 2007?

5. What are the Webographics of our customer base, and how are those factors changing?

6. Do we know why our customers behave the way they do?

7. How well do we know our individual customers' changing needs?

8. Which e-communities do our customers participate in and

how might we best reach them?

9. What things are we *not* doing that our customers would like us to do?

10. Can we be open for business 24 × 7 × 365 on a worldwide basis?

11. As the Web goes wireless, where and how will our customers want to buy from us?

12. What experience are we delivering to our customers and how might we enhance it?

13. How can we extract more value from our customer database?

14. Which are our most valuable customer groups; what do they most value?

15. How do we obtain and retain customer loyalty?

16. How can we improve our customer feedback systems?

17. Can we stop advertising?

18. How might we exploit word of modem and affiliate marketing?

19. In what ways might we best sell the Web Lifestyle?

20. How might we best e-brand ourselves?

21. How might we optimize customer service in the Internet Age?

22. How do we ensure that our website gets bookmarked onto "Favorites" lists?

INDEX

advertising, 14, 24, 31, 43, 108, 138
  Amazon, 14, 24, 31
  classified, 42, 47, 48
  eBay and, 14
  Quixtar, 84, 89
  Tesco and, 114
Albertson's, 121, 122
Amazon, 18, 102, 131, 141
  advertising, 14, 24, 31
  and auctions, 41
  brand, 33, 34, 36, 37
  content and, 24, 25, 35, 36
  customers, 31, 32
  customization, 24, 25–26, 33,
    35, 36, 139
  distribution system, 26–27
  and eBay, 43, 74, 75
  first-mover advantage, 22–23,
    33, 34
  history, 22–23, 26, 29, 33
  inventory, 32, 35
  investment mistakes by, 29
  market share, 15, 137
  net profits, 33
  ordering system, 25–26, 35
  partnerships, 29–31, 35
  pricing, 31–32, 35
  product range, 28–29, 35, 110
  sales, 27, 32–33, 34, 136, 137
  Services, 29
  shipping costs, 31
apparel, 42, 98, 99, 100
appliances, 96, 99
ASDA, 123
auctions, online, 29, 40, 43, 46
  and Amazon, 41
  and Yahoo, 41
  See also eBay
automation, 16, 67, 139
  in distribution, 26–27, 82, 115
  in manufacturing, 61
  in ordering, 76–77, 115
automobiles, 42, 47

Barnes & Noble, 27, 137
Bass, Bill, 98. See also Sears Roebuck

Bezos, Jeff, 22, 23–24, 26, 33
  on pricing, 31
  See also Amazon
Biznets, 130, 132, 136
bookmarks. See Favorites list
books, 28, 30, 137
  on eBay, 42
  online sale of, 11, 25, 33, 136
  See also Amazon
Borders Books, 30, 137
brand, 14, 17, 33
  Amazon, 33, 34, 36, 37
  eBay, 14, 54
  experience, 16, 37, 53, 139–41
  extension, 25, 28, 124
  loyalty, 54
  names, 47
  offline, 141
  online, 36
  private-label, 111
  recognition, 52
Brazil, 19
broadband, 12, 33, 34
Browett, John, 108, 117
Butterfield & Butterfield, 46

Canada, 75
  catalog shopping in, 92–93
  online shopping in, 94
capital, "social," 44, 52, 54, 139
catalogs, 104, 124, 137
  eBay and, 50–51, 53
  Sears and, 92–93, 96–97
  Tesco and, 115
category management, 43, 53
China, 19
clothing. See apparel
Cohen, Jack, 111. See also Tesco
collaborative filtering, 26, 36
collaborative planning, forecasting, and
  replenishment (CPFR), 101, 103
collectibles, 42, 43
community, 40, 44, 45–46, 54, 55
competition, 130, 132
  barrier to, 34
computers, 10, 11, 12, 42, 59, 137

content, 53, 125
  Amazon and, 24, 25, 35, 36
  as product, 13, 25, 35, 132, 136
  customers as, 36
  multimedia, 103, 132
  See also website
Craigslist, 47
credit cards, 26, 44, 97
critical mass, 34, 53, 124, 132
CRM. See customer relationship management
cross-channel
  marketing, 101
  shopping, 96, 103
cross-docking, 118
cross-selling, 25, 35, 41, 126, 137
  Tesco and, 113
customer relationship management
  (CRM), 104, 126, 133, 139
  Dell and, 64, 65
  Quixtar and, 82, 89
  Sears and, 96–97, 101
  Tesco and,112–13
customers
  Amazon, 31, 32
  brand experience of, 17, 139
  brick-n-mortar, 19
  high-value, 127
  loyalty of, 132, 138
    programs promoting,112, 127
  online, 19, 31, 32, 138
  self-service by, 138
  service, 23, 26
customization, 13, 19, 45, 132, 138, 140
  Amazon and, 24, 25–26, 33, 35,
    36, 139
  Dell and, 65–67, 69, 71
  mass, 16, 25, 27, 58, 136
  See also personalization

delivery, 132
  charges, 31, 116
  free, 100, 104, 126
  home 19, 120
  Tesco and,112
Dell, 18, 131, 132, 139, 141
  cash flow, 63, 70
  customer support, 67–68, 71
  customization, 65–67, 69, 71
  employee training, 62, 70

feedback, 65, 72
  first-mover advantage of, 69
  history of, 58–59
  inventory, 62–63
  localization and, 60, 70
  manufacturing, 60–62
  market segmentation, 64–66
  market share, 59, 68–69
  outsourcing, 68, 71
  product range, 63–64
  profit, 58
  sales, 59
  suppliers, 59–60, 62–63
  websites, 60, 71
Dell, Michael, 57, 58, 65
distribution, 24, 26, 121, 124
  Amazon and, 26–27
  centers, 95, 102, 108, 117, 118
  Quixtar and, 27
  scalability, 27
  systems, 27
  Tesco and,115
  See also delivery; order fulfillment

Eaton's, 92
eBay, 18, 131, 136
  advertising, and, 14
  Amazon and, 43, 74, 75
  branding and, 14, 54
  brick-n-mortar presence of, 50
  category management and, 43–44
  classified advertising and, 47–48
  community, 45–46, 54, 55
  customer base, 15, 40, 41, 46
  economic cycles and, 51–52
  in Europe, 41
  feedback and, 44–45
  first-mover advantage of, 29, 40–42
  gross merchandise volume, 15, 42
  history of, 40–41, 48, 49, 141
  investment mistakes by, 46
  in Japan, 41
  licensing by, 49, 53
  localization by, 50, 53
  marketing by, 50–51
  Motors, 42, 47
  multi-channel expansion of, 50
  payment service, 48, 50
  pricing by, 49–50, 54
  product range, 42–43

profits of, 40, 51
Quixtar and, 74, 75
"social capital" and, 52
in South Korea, 41
start-up costs of, 48
Stores, 43
strategic partnerships, 46–47, 53
training and, 46
as Webopoly, 42
Webpreneurs and, 45–46, 52, 54, 133
website, 48–49
Yahoo and, 41
electronics, consumer, 28, 42, 111

Favorites lists, 36, 55, 140
branding and, 16, 24
feedback, 44–45, 54, 65, 72, 139
first-mover advantage, 22, 34, 130
Amazon and, 22–23, 33, 34
Dell and, 69
eBay and, 29, 40–42
Tesco and, 108, 109

Gates, Bill, 10, 131
glocal, 14, 50, 53, 60, 133
Tesco and,115
See also localization
groceries, 77, 108, 110, 123
shopping online for, 108
GroceryWorks.com, 122
guarantees, 36

Half.com, 49
high-touch, 15, 45, 113, 139
home workers, 35, 95, 104, 125
home-based businesses, 14, 46, 53.
See also Webpreneurs
HomeGrocer.com, 29

IBM, 59
India, 19
information technology (IT), 101, 131
Internet, 10, 26, 35, 104, 137, 141
economies of scale, 25, 35
"frictionless economics" of, 40
network effect, 52
inventory, 14, 25, 31, 43, 61, 132, 136
Amazon and, 32, 35
Dell and, 62–63

Japan, 19, 41, 47

Kijiji, 48
Kmart, 102

Lands' End, 30, 100
Sears and, 92, 97–99, 101, 102, 104
languages, 94, 104
late-movers, 103, 124
licensing, 29, 35, 49, 53, 124
LiveBid.com, 29
localization, 94, 104, 136
by Dell, 60, 70
by eBay, 48, 50
in pricing, 126
in product range, 125
See also glocal
logistics, 35, 102, 103, 126, 137

manufacturing, 60–62
market domination, 11, 52, 140
marketing, 43, 53, 133
affiliate/network, 76, 79, 82, 85, 87,
88, 133
by eBay, 50–51
permission/"opt-in," 16
segmentation, 64–66, 113
"6 Ps" of, 15, 136
test-,101, 103
Marketplaats, 47
McLuhan, Marshall, 13, 23
Metcalfe's Law of networks, 12, 138
Moore's Law, 11
music sales online, 28, 42

Omidyar, Pierre, 40
order, 25–26, 35, 125
fulfillment, 14, 19, 26, 36, 95,
101, 115, 116, 137
picking, 102, 115–16, 119–20, 127
size online, 32
tracking, 95
outsourcing, 30, 68, 71

partnerships, strategic, 33, 53, 58,
122, 125, 130, 132
with Amazon, 29–31, 35
with eBay, 47
with Quixtar, 79
with Tesco, 112

PayPal, 48, 50
PCs (personal computers), 10, 11, 12, 42, 59, 137
Peapod, 109, 121, 122
personalization, 19, 36, 54, 140
  Amazon and, 24–25, 33
  CRM and, 101, 139
  customer service and, 15, 16
  Tesco and, 113
  See also customization; high-touch
pick-up/return centers, 53, 96, 104, 136
portals, 29, 31, 47
PowerSellers, 46
pricing, 31–32, 35, 49–50, 54
  comparisons, 31, 96, 126, 138
  competitive, 31
  Dynamic Value, 16
  fixed, 49, 50
  Quixtar and, 79, 80, 88
  Tesco and, 112, 126
produce, 119, 120
product range, 13, 15, 31, 35, 43, 103, 111, 125
profit
  net, 40, 51, 58
  of Amazon, 33
  of eBay, 40, 51
  sharing, 119, 127
profitability, 17, 23, 33, 124

Quixtar, 18, 131, 133, 139, 141
  advertising, 84, 89
  affiliate marketing and, 76, 79, 82, 85, 86, 87, 88
  distribution, 27
  "Ditto" delivery, 74, 76–77, 84, 88
  and eBay, 74, 75
  independent business owners (IBOs), 74, 76, 77–78, 80, 82
  market share, 75
  membership, 76
  Partner Stores, 79
  pricing, 79, 80, 88
  product range, 78–79
  promotions, 83–84
  recruitment, 85–86
  sales, 74
  start up of, 74–75, 82, 87
  training, 81
  website, 75–76

radio frequency identification (RFID), 117, 124
Rakuten, 19, 41
real estate, 27, 42
retailing
  big-box, 24, 32, 79, 82, 131
  brick-n-mortar, 19, 22, 27, 30, 50, 97, 136
  click-and-mortar, 27, 53, 103, 123, 131
  multi-channel, 50, 51, 95–97, 101, 103, 133
  integration of, 27, 98, 103, 136
  online, 28, 96, 103, 117, 125, 131

retirees, 120, 125
returns of purchases, 31, 95, 100

Safeway, 118, 121, 122
Sainsbury's, 109, 110
sales, 27, 28, 32, 59
  Amazon and, 32, 34
  in-store, 96
  Tesco and, 110
scalability, 27, 40, 53, 126
search engines, 35, 53, 103
Sears Canada, 92–94, 102
  customers, 95, 96
  multi-channel approach, 95–97, 103
  online channel (Sears.ca), 92–94
  website design, 94–95
Sears Roebuck, 18, 92, 131, 133, 141
  catalogs and, 92–93
  distribution, 101–02
  Kmart and, 102
  Lands' End and, 92, 97–99, 101, 102, 104
  logistics, 102, 103
  product range, 99–100
  website design, 94, 96, 97, 98–99, 100–01
shipping. *See* delivery; order fulfillment
shopping lists
  Quixtar and, 74, 76–77, 84, 88
  Tesco and, 115
Sotheby's, 47
South Korea, 41, 118
start-up
  "Big Bang," 133
  costs, 48
  of eBay, 48

of Tesco.com, 115
fast-growth strategy, 23
of Quixtar, 74–75, 82, 87
size, 34, 52
speed of, 137
Submarino, 19
supermarkets, 121, 123. *See also* Tesco.
suppliers, 32, 58, 132
   Dell and, 59–60, 62–63
   Tesco and, 114

television, in-house, 113–15, 111, 119
Tesco, 18, 108, 116, 118, 131, 133, 141
   advertising, 114
   catalogs, 115, 124
   competitors of, 123
   cross-selling, 113, 126
   customer base, 109, 110, 116, 120
   customer relations management
      (CRM), 113, 126
   distribution, 115–16, 117–18
   financial services, 112
   history, 109, 110, 111, 117
   localization 115, 125, 126
   loyalty program, 112–13
   market segmentation and, 112–13
   multi-channel selling, 131
   multimedia, 114, 125, 126
   online start-up, 115, 117
   order-fulfillment, 115, 125
   perishables, 119–20
   personalized coupons, 113
   pricing, 112, 126
   product range, 110–11
   profit-sharing, 119
   Safeway and, 122
   sales, 110
   shopping list, 115
   strategic partners of, 112, 122
   training, 118–19, 127
   TV, 113–15, 111, 119
"touch and feel," 103, 120, 125
ToysRUs, 29–30
training, employee/user, 101, 104
   Dell and, 62, 70
   eBay and, 46

Quixtar and, 81
Tesco and, 118–19, 127

value web, 16, 60
video sales online, 28, 42
virtual reality, 99, 104

Wal-Mart, 22–23, 32, 82, 123, 131, 137
   online, 18, 22, 75, 98, 100, 102
warehouses, 26
Web Lifestyle, 10, 45
Webolution, 10, 15, 130, 141
Webopoly, 10, 102, 132, 141, 142
   commercial impact, 11, 14, 130, 131
   eBay as, 40, 42
Webpreneurs, 14, 43, 53, 141
   eBay and, 45–46, 52, 54, 133
   Quixtar and, 74, 76, 77–78, 80, 82
website, 13, 100, 101, 110, 140
   Dell, 60, 71
   eBay, 48–49
   content, 24, 28, 98, 139
   design, 15
   links, 30, 98, 101
   Quixtar, 75–76
   Sears.ca, 94–95
   Sears.com, 94, 96, 97, 98–99, 100–01
   Tesco, 110
   traffic, 27, 33, 49
   user-friendliness of, 13
Webvan, 108, 109, 123
Whitman, Meg, 44. *See also* eBay.
wireless, 12, 26, 48, 102, 115
wish lists, 25, 95
word of modem, 17, 19, 24, 36, 40, 55,
   138
word of mouth, 48, 83, 84, 138
   See also marketing, affiliate/network
working-from-home trend, 35, 95, 104,
   125

Yahoo, 29, 47
   eBay and, 41

zero–infinity, 11, 14, 15, 142
zShops, 29

ABOUT THE AUTHOR

Frank Feather is a global business futurist and strategist, corporate director, best-selling author, and an in-demand keynote speaker and seminar leader.

In 1979 he coined the now well-known phrase, "Thinking Globally, Acting Locally," which he converged in 1993 to create the "glocal" concept. He is ranked by Macmillan's *Encyclopedia of the Future* (1996) as one of the "Top 100 Futurists of All Time," a list that includes Leonardo da Vinci.

In 1980, Frank organized and was Chairman and Director General of the "First Global Conference on the Future," sponsored by the World Future Society, Washington, DC. Still the largest conference of its kind ever held, it drew 6,000 attendees from 56 countries and had more than 1,000 speakers over a five-day program of multifarious topics.

Formerly a strategic planning executive with three of the world's biggest banks — Barclays, TD, and CIBC — in 1981 Frank founded Toronto-based Glocal Marketing Consultants and Future-Trends.com. He consults across all industries to global firms such as Ford, GM, IBM, Nokia, and Shell. As well, he has advised the IMF/World Bank, the United Nations, and the governments of the United States, Canada, and Mexico. He has been a Special Advisor to the Chinese government on economic modernization and market reform since 1984. Even the world's big consulting firms regularly pick his brain.

Mr. Feather's 1989 book *G-Forces: The 35 Global Forces Restructuring Our Future* met wide acclaim in the USA, Canada, and Japan. His 1993 book *The Future Consumer* was re-issued in 1997 due to popular demand and also was published in Chinese. His *Future Consumer.Com* (2000) was on the best-seller list at Amazon.com for many weeks. More recent books include *Future Living* (2002) and *Futuristic Leadership A-Z* (2004).

To Contact Frank Feather for Speaking Engagements or Consulting Assignments,

please e-mail him at: Biznets@Hotmail.com